Bright Minds, Poor Grades

D0107175

Most Perigee Books are available at special quantity discounts for bulk purchases for sales promotions, premiums, fund-raising or educational use. Special books, or book excerpts, can also be created to fit specific needs.

For details, write: Special Markets, The Berkley Publishing Group, 375 Hudson Street, New York, New York 10014.

Bright Minds, Poor Grades

Michael D. Whitley, Ph.D.

A Perigee Book

A Perigee Book
Published by The Berkley Publishing Group
A division of Penguin Putnam Inc.
375 Hudson Street
New York, New York 10014

Copyright © 2001 by Michael D. Whitley, Ph.D.
Text design by Tiffany Kukec
Cover design by Jill Boltin
Cover photos of teenage boy at table copyright © by Robert Burke/Stone
Cover photo of schoolgirl at desk copyright © by Penny Tweedie/Stone
Author photo by Karen Elaine Harrison, Ray Sakers Photography,
Houston, Texas

All rights reserved. This book, or parts thereof, may not be reproduced in any
form without permission.

First edition: July 2001
Published simultaneously in Canada.

The Penguin Putnam Inc. World Wide Web site address is
www.penguinputnam.com

Library of Congress Cataloging-in-Publication Data
Whitley, Michael D.
Bright minds, poor grades : understanding and motivating your underachieving
child / Michael D. Whitley.
    p. cm.
Originally published: Houston, Tex.: Whitley Group, c1996.
Includes index.
ISBN 0-399-52705-2
1. Parenting. 2. Underachievers. 3. Achievement motivation in children. 4.
Academic achievement. 5. Education—Parent participation. 6. Motivation
in education. I. Title.
HQ755.8 . W485 2001
370.15'4—dc21   00-053732

Printed in the United States of America
10 9 8 7 6 5 4 3 2 1

To Marilyn and my children
Todd, Katharine, and Allison

Contents

Introduction

Parents: What is wrong when your capable child brings home more bad grades and more poor report cards? He is intelligent enough to do better, but he consistently underachieves due to a lack of responsibility, excuses for failures, and a lack of motivation and effort to achieve. He seems lazy and disinterested in success and nothing seems to help. Year after year he is not growing out of it, and may even be getting worse. He seems to be a good kid, but he does not follow through on his promises to "do better next time," and astonishingly, he even rejects a helping hand when he needs it the most. What is wrong here?

Your child may be an underachiever. If you knew what caused him to make poor grades and fail to reach his potential, maybe you could be a more effective parent, and maybe, your child could learn to be more motivated and successful. As it stands now, he is simply closing doors to his future. And he may not even be interested in discussing his future seriously.

Over the years in my work, I have seen parents become frustrated, angry, and discouraged by their bright but underachieving children. I've seen parents resent and worry over their underachieving children's deceptions, lies, manipulations, and work themselves to exhaustion trying to motivate their children to become successful. I have seen parents try one home remedy after another, from tutoring to power tactics, groundings and punishments, lectures and pleading, and even leaving kids alone to suffer failures on their own . . . to no avail. Sometimes, an inspired parent will spark the fires of motivation in their children, only to see the promise of sustained success flicker briefly in the dark and then be snuffed out. I have seen bewildered and angry parents demand "why?" and get for their trouble only a shrug of their children's shoulders and a vacuously inadequate "I don't know" for an answer.

Bright children who fail or underachieve in school are a sad puzzle. Parents try to motivate them but nothing seems to help. When they reach the teenage years, from seventh grade onward, many adolescent underachievers begin to have other problems. Family conflicts and tensions escalate and depression and low self-esteem set in and some children turn to drugs, alcohol, or promiscuity to escape the cumulative pain of their failures. They substitute pleasure seeking for their lack of independence, confidence, and the deep pride that comes from successful work. Through these years of struggle from childhood to adolescence, parents begin to worry. Time slips by and a quietly disparate thought gnaws remorselessly at the heart: "A long pattern of self-defeat is emerging that will rob my child of happiness. My child defeats himself in school, how will he be able to get along in life later on? Will he defeat himself then as he does now? Is there nothing I can do to help?"

Why do bright kids underachieve or get into trouble? The answers are to be sought in their deepest values.

Basic human values are involved in the problems of success and underachievement. These values are too important to quality of life and even the continued prosperity of our country to be ignored or treated by trivial and ultimately impotent success techniques that promise quick, magical cures for long-term problems. These quality-of-life values are the foundation of character, and without them sustained success in work and family is impossible. These character values involve such old-fashioned but irreplaceable virtues as self-discipline, commitment to goals, the ability to sacrifice momentary pleasures for the greater rewards of tomorrow, independence in motivation, moral responsibility, cooperative effort, trust, the capacity to govern oneself, and an abiding commitment to family and the development of one's own talent. Students who sustain achievement in school almost always reflect these old-fashioned values in their behavior. Underachieving students who have brains but lack effort almost always reflect a lack of these old-fashioned virtues in their behavior. Because their efforts miss these virtues, underachievers almost always suffer from a lack of emotional meaning in life. They lose the power and pleasures work could bring to them.

The true emotional power of work is to make life meaningful for the individual and his community. With the right attitudes and commitments, work can transform individuals and bring joy to life. The recognition of the importance and power of work stretches deeply into the historical and spiritual roots of our civilization. In the Bible, for example, the ability to love and work plays a crucial role in the development of a worth-while life. Loss of the capacity to love labor leaves individuals in such despair that one Biblical author admonishes his readers that, "Whatsoever thy hand findeth to do, do it with all thy might," and "There is nothing better for a man than that he would eat and drink, and that he should make his soul enjoy good in his labour." (Ecclesiastes 9:10 and Ecclesiastes 2:24).

It is not merely an accident of language that the author of Ecclesiastes makes the verb *enjoy* into an act of trained will. If we do not make our hearts enjoy the tasks before us, then it is no one else's responsibility to bring us enjoyment in our work. Achievers are usually able to wring some pleasure out of even the most tedious of tasks. It is sadly a fact of experience that underachievers almost always find ways to resent and hate having to do work. When they do work, it is usually only when the mood strikes. If they have an especially entertaining teacher, or if they happen to like what they are learning, they work, but only until their feelings change . . . then they fail once more. There is a passivity in their approach to life and work. They do not, indeed, they believe they cannot, learn to control their own feelings to find a way to "make their soul enjoy the good in their labor." Something must motivate them from the outside, must push or pull them to achieve. On their own they fail. Their potential festers like an old, unhealed, self-inflicted wound that they refuse to see they have the ultimate power to heal.

There is nothing better a parent can do than to teach his children how to develop that inner will to succeed, to connect enjoyment and positive feelings to tasks, to learn to work with all their might, and learn to motivate themselves from within.

If children are always waiting for something magic to happen to them before they learn how to work, then they will likely waste their time waiting around for something to happen, hoping someone, somewhere, will do something vital for them. This is the hope of a wasted life.

Emotionally healthy individuals have two great powers at their disposal: these are the power to love and the power to work. All underachievers lack emotional health when it comes to work. They cannot consistently perform work. If children cannot learn to work, then they will eventually suffer from other problems as well, such as depression, anxiety, unhealthy dependency on others, and finding substitutes for a meaningful life such as substance abuse and promiscuity, all of which lead children to a sense of victimhood and boredom that is so prevalent in our country today.

Sometimes underachievers suffer from an incapacity to sustain love and passion for relationships as well. Love is the ability to live in cooperative relationships with others, to listen and learn from people who are more experienced or knowledgeable, to feel empathy and compassion for others, and to sustain effort to make one's heart love and understand those with whom we daily live and work.

The power to love and work and the ability to combine these two powers of life into one's daily routines: these are the needs of underachieving children. Their inability to combine and control love and work ultimately lead to their troubles and the impotency of most strategies parents use to help them grow. To truly help underachievers, all changes in tactics need to focus on the child's developing character and deepest values. Love and work are the essence of mental health, the essence of growing up, and the bedrock, essential values on which this book is based.

The techniques I provide in this book for helping bright but underachieving children are in every sense of the word, *disciplines*. That is to say, they have to be assimilated and must become part of the fabric of an individual parent's judgment and perception. An individual must grow into them over time and use. Then, when the techniques are followed consistently, with passion and commitment, change almost always follows. As always, positive change arises from the growth that the disciplines in this book produce in the parent-child relationship, in the maturation of the child's character, and in the personal and family issues being addressed.

In all my years of working with underachievers, I have learned that making changes in study behavior and raising grades are relatively easy and straightforward, given some intellectual talent and the willpower to sustain persistence and follow through. Training the character of a child to allow him to increase willpower and overcome self-defeating habits is difficult and time consuming. It takes time and care because the path to character change is rarely straight. It is a winding, crooked path that often turns on itself and takes unexpected plunges and twists, with promising avenues coming unexpectedly to dead ends, and seeming dead ends leading unexpectedly to rich insights and maturational growths. The disciplines taught in this book are best thought of as methods to keep on the right path to change no matter how crooked and dark the path becomes.

However, I advise a word of caution. As parents, we feed

our children's problems in the most subtle ways and rarely do we understand how we do that. Parents and children form very complex emotional and behavioral patterns in their families, and when there are chronic difficulties, the parent's own impulses to impose various disciplines and rules may be the very things that maintain the existence of the difficulties they are trying to change.

This book will provide parents with the first critical elements necessary for change: clarity and understanding. This book will help parents understand the nature of underachievement and what causes it to occur in otherwise good and intelligent kids. It will help parents understand what they must do properly to set the stage for real change to begin. It will help parents understand the purpose and goals involved in the disciplines and techniques for creating change. Finally, this book will explain the techniques that I have found to be powerful tools for helping children take over their own lives and change their destiny for the better.

Real, lasting change is what is sought in these pages. Lasting change requires a coming together of a multitude of elements in an individual and a family. Not all of the ingredients of change will be evident and predictable at the beginning of effort. No book, not even mine, can substitute completely for the help parents can receive in counseling on these problems, especially when the psychotherapist understands the issues involved in underachievement and takes these issues seriously.

Finally, parents will need skills to put this book to best use. These skills are not easily taught, for they involve virtues and values inherent in an individual's character. These skills are a capacity for empathy, compassion, and patience; an ability to listen intently for what a child says and what a child leaves unsaid; an ability to be persistent over time and follow through even when angry or discouraged. It requires a capacity to sustain the search for truth and honesty in relationships. Above all, it requires a passionate capacity to sustain love for someone who may be angry, rejecting, and resentful when you are being understanding and rational. If you do not have these skills or have trouble maintaining them under stress—and if you try to change a chronic underachiever, you will experience stress—then go to a professional familiar with chronic underachievement, who can help you develop and maintain these skills. You will need that person.

I wish you luck, love, and good fortune.

*Bright Minds,
Poor Grades*

Part I

The Problem

Chapter 1

Meet Three Underachievers

A Nice Young Man

I first met John when he was sixteen years old. His parents sent him to my office because he was failing in school and had a history of lack of motivation and underachievement.

I saw John sitting in my waiting room, and he certainly made an impression. When he saw me open the door, he stood up and walked toward me. He wore a well-groomed look of jeans and polo shirt and loafers. He was about six feet tall. He looked like an all-American kid.

As he approached me he extended his hand for me to shake and smiled warmly. "Hi!" he said. "I'm John, and you must be Dr. Whitley. My parents sent me here to get some motivation."

I pointed the way to my office. When he entered, John did not pause for a moment like most people, waiting for me to invite them to the appropriate seat. John simply surveyed my office and promptly sat down in my chair. It was rather obvious it was my chair because my glasses, notepad, and a cup of coffee were on the table beside the chair. John waited patiently for me to take a seat. I sat on the couch.

John's apparent lack of anxiety and easy informality and charm were actually clues to the causes of John's underachievement problems. John was telling me he was used to being in charge of adults and that he would subtly resist being interviewed by me regarding his problems in school. He made it clear initially that he had come passively to "get some motivation," which I was somehow going to supply for him. In his own mind he definitely was not seeing me to learn how to become more responsible for himself and learn to control his own motivation.

Both of John's parents were successful. His father was an attorney and his mother was a former model. They had two other children, an older daughter and a younger son, both of whom did very well in school and sports.

In their first meeting with me, both parents agreed John was a good kid, well liked by teachers and peers, and, they emphasized, he was especially popular with the girls. "They call him at all hours," his mother explained. John's parents expressed general comfort with his friends. In fact, the father felt that John's social charm was an asset and that he would make a good salesman someday, "if he ever finishes school."

Both parents felt that John was the smartest of their three children. The other two made superior grades because they worked harder than John. "He could do well with so little effort," his mother lamented. "He's lazy," his father joined in. "He wants good grades, but he doesn't want to put out the effort for them."

The sixth grade was the beginning of a long downward spiral

for John. Homework was counted more and more as part of John's grades and more effort was required for him to keep up. His grades took a nosedive because he did not do much homework or study much at home. "Why should I have to do homework when I know the stuff already?" John complained. He seemingly ignored his parents' logic that homework was required, and he was only hurting himself by not turning it in. John also complained that some teachers picked on him or were unfair. Yet, the teachers said he was charming and they just wanted him to do his work.

John's grades yo-yoed from As to Fs, sometimes in the same class during a single grading period. Although he managed to maintain passing averages, his performance was so inconsistent and so poor overall that his parents decided to make him study. Since his father worked so much, it fell to his mother to make sure he did better in school.

Every school day, John's mother asked questions about school assignments. Sometimes John told the truth, many times he told lies such as having done his homework at school or not having any at all. The more his mother tried to become involved, the more memory problems John seemed to develop. He had forgotten to turn in assignments she had made sure he had done at an A-quality level the night before. She would help him organize his notebook, only to find it in chaos again a few days later. When she tried to help him prepare for exams, he would become sullen and resistant to the point where she would angrily rebuke his irresponsible attitudes and behavior. To get some relief, she sent John to tutoring for help. He did well with the tutoring program. Unfortunately, he remained unmotivated in school. Despite all she could do, John actually began to fail some classes. Further, the resentments between John and his mother increased steadily until she dreaded his coming home from school and longed for the sixth grade year to be over. Summer would be a relief!

At the very end of the sixth grade, John was told by two teachers that he had to make high grades on his finals to pass. John did well on his exams and passed by the skin of his teeth.

A school psychologist was consulted at the end of the school year. The school psychologist saw John once and reviewed John's progress in school with him. In a meeting with the parents later, the school psychologist told them that John was a normal young man and that all he needed was more discipline and motivation. He assured the parents that John would grow out of his problems, eventually. However, teachers and the school counselor recommended that John's parents consider holding him back a year to let him mature. He was not ready for the seventh grade. Doubtful but hopeful, John's parents assented. He was held back for one year.

John only slightly resisted his parents' decision. As he pointed out to them, he placed above grade level on achievement tests, which proved he had already learned his sixth grade material. "So why hold me back?" he argued.

At the end of the repeated sixth grade year, John's grades had not improved much. He talked and clowned in class, forgot homework, was disorganized in his notebooks, and family tensions between John and his parents were as bad as ever. He was still popular and well-liked, but he remained unmotivated and seemingly as disinterested in success as the year before. A teacher remarked to John's mother at the end of the repeated year, "I think we made a mistake holding John back."

As the years ebbed away, John and his parents continued to struggle in school. Bribes and punishments for grades, making deals for homework performed, lectures by the father, more tutoring: all were to no avail. John never again failed a school year. Sometimes, when he had a particularly good teacher, he would do much better. Otherwise, he survived on promises to do better, parental involvement, and last-ditch efforts. Although his parents thought about placing John in counseling, he basically seemed a happy young man away from school. He was not involved with drugs nor had serious problems with authority.

By the tenth grade, however, John began to fail classes for the first time since the sixth grade. His parents were out of answers. The only answers frustrated school officials offered were unacceptable; just let him continue to fail and hope he grows out of it someday.

As I sat silently and looked at John sitting across from me, I considered the history his parents had given me. I let him speak. He showed no signs of anxiety, but looked about my office and commented on one of my paintings. Finally, I asked him about algebra. "I noticed you failed algebra last year and you are failing it this year, too. Do you know why?"

He shifted in the chair to a more alert and upright position. "You know, I'm glad you asked that question."

He explained how he had been bored with math last year, but this year he really wanted to do well. However, his algebra teacher did not "explain things right." John said that she was a nice person, but he just couldn't relate to her. "Besides, it's too hard to concentrate in that class. It's hot in the room. It's my fourth period, after lunch, and I'm too full, I guess, so I get sleepy."

I said nothing. John was full of excuses. He then told me how at the beginning of the year he had wanted to transfer to another class down the hall, where his friends were. However, "the stupid counselor" would not transfer John and would not even listen to his parents.

"But I was thinking," John added, "maybe you could help me."

"How?"

"Well, since you're a doctor, I'll bet you have more pull than me or my parents. You could write a doctor's excuse for me to get to the other class. They'd have to transfer me then. I'm sure I could do better in algebra if you'd write that letter."

I knew whose fault it would be if John continued to fail algebra. It would be my fault, because I had no intention of doing all those things for him. Later on, I learned that John had told his parents that they were just wasting their money because I couldn't help him since I would not write that letter for him.

The Silent Child

The Petersons were bright and articulate parents, and they were clearly upset in telling me about their daughter, Alice. Teachers had always told the Petersons that Alice was capable of making excellent grades. Initially in school, she was shy and had a few friends outside of the family, but was a voracious reader and an A student. When she was twelve years old in the sixth grade, her marks began to suffer due to missed assignments, forgetfulness, and carelessness. She became more disorganized and sloppy in her work. The Petersons had never pressured their daughter into good grades as she had always been a responsible and seemingly well-motivated student.

In the seventh grade, Alice began to become more popular. She was invited to parties and even had a boyfriend. Mr. Peterson felt her socializing was a good sign of maturity. Yet, in school, Alice's grades did not improve. Alice seemed angry with herself and with her parents, and at times expressed her frustrations in a temper that was unusual for her. She worked hard and pulled her grades up sufficiently to make a B average by the end of the first semester. By the second semester, however, Alice nearly failed two important academic subjects: math and science.

The Petersons tried to help. At first, they believed the teachers did not like their daughter and would pick on her sometimes. On the other hand, teachers complained that Alice daydreamed in her classes, rarely participated in class discussions, and turned in work late or incomplete. Sometimes she disrupted classes with her socializing. Tensions between Alice and her parents, especially between her and her mother, increased noticeably throughout the seventh grade.

In the eighth grade, the Petersons could no longer blame the school. Alice began to tell lies about having done homework at school or having none to do. She spent more and more time alone in her room listening to music or watching television or talking on the telephone to her new friends. She began to hide her grades from her parents. On report cards, her grades were uneven at best—sometimes As and sometimes Fs. She would promise to do better, but would lack follow-through. She said she wanted to do well, but would work mainly when supervised by her mother. Sometimes, Alice would do excellent work at home, but fail to turn it in the next day in class. When confronted by angry and puzzled parents, Alice would make one excuse after another for almost every failure or shortcoming. Sometimes she would sit in silence, eyes tearing, and say nothing or just shrug her shoulders.

School became a struggle between Alice and her parents. Numerous efforts to correct the problem of poor grades and motivation were tried with little success. Alice's father had her tutored and trained in a study skills program. She still lacked the will to make As. Neither her grades nor her behavior improved much.

Mrs. Peterson talked to her daughter on numerous occasions, and Alice seemed to understand how good grades were important to her future. She sincerely wanted to go to a good college. She would promise to do better. She would work harder for a couple of weeks, but then her resolve, like New Year's resolutions, would fail her and her grades would fall once more.

Following the advice of the school counselor, the Petersons began a program of reward for good grades and punishment for poor grades. They explained the rules quite carefully to Alice. Everything made sense. The "real" world was run by rewards and punishments, so if the parents ran their relationship with Alice the same way, certainly Alice would do better.

The Petersons began their new program at the end of the eighth grade, with good results. Alice managed to pull up her grades and pass all of her courses with a C average or better. The Petersons repeated the new program in the ninth grade with equally good results at first. However, by Thanksgiving, Alice had made two more Fs. She had also become more hostile and resentful toward her parents' rules. She avoided the simple things they asked of her and withdrew more from the family. Sometimes, Alice would not talk to them for days.

The Petersons felt they were losing their daughter. Where had that young girl gone whom they had been so proud of in the first years of school? Finally, Alice's parents became even more worried. She seemed tired and listless at home, and her teachers had begun to report that she was sleeping in some of her classes.

One day, when Alice had reached the tenth grade, the high school counselor suggested that the Petersons quit trying so hard to help Alice in school. The counselor advised them to let Alice fail on her own. Then, she would suffer the consequences of her own actions and learn to do better as a result of experience. The Petersons backed off entirely. They did not even mention school to Alice, even though they were still very worried about her.

The next six weeks, Alice failed three of her major subjects and barely passed the others. Alice's highest grade was in physical education. When they tried to talk with her, Alice would sit staring vacantly in an angry stony silence. The Petersons could not stand idly by and watch their daughter continue to fail. But what could they do next to help her? The Petersons were out of answers and Alice was not talking.

The Talk Show Host

A tall, attractive man in his mid-forties was a host on a live radio interview show on a small, nonprofit station. He hosted the show without pay and was on the air talking with me about underachievement. He startled me with his candor. He told me that when he had first heard me speak, he knew that he had to have me on his show. He told me he had been fighting underachievement and self-defeat for most of his life due to his perfectionism. "I'm fighting it every day I live," he said.

He told me how he grew up with "all the advantages." His mother was well-educated and his father was a very successful dental surgeon. His family was blessed with plenty of money and material goods, but "I just never caught on," he said. "All my life I looked up to my father and admired him from afar. But I never thought I could get his approval." The talk show host told me how he had failed the fifth and seventh grades and felt "stupid" despite having been told as a child that he possessed superior intelligence. "My mother wanted me to be successful like my father," he continued. He elaborated how he had carried a burden inside of being a disappointment to his father all of his early life. "I went to college," he said. "But I dropped out. From the fifth grade on, no matter how hard I tried, I just never felt I'd ever be good enough."

The radio show continued with further disclosures by the host. He spoke openly of the discouragement he felt regarding himself and his life. Since his late high school years, he had wanted to be in broadcast journalism, but was forced by his self-defeating failures eventually to work in a retail store to support his family. He worked without pay at the radio station just to have a taste of his heart's desire.

I remember clearly the pain in his eyes as he summed up the broadcast hour. He said he believed his father may have really accepted and loved him all along. But his father had recently died before he had had a chance to talk with him about their relationship. "I wish this thing would have been taken care of a long time ago when I was young," he said. Then he told his radio audience, "If you are listening out there and understand what you have heard this hour, take care of perfectionism and underachievement now, before the sands of time run out on you and the ones you love."

John, Alice, and the Talk Show Host are underachievers. They were bright enough, they had the talent, they often felt regret and guilt over their failures and wished to do better. Yet, over and over these individuals arranged defeat for themselves as though they had some strange attraction to failure. They failed despite what their parents and teachers did to help them. Parents begged, pleaded, grounded, trained, pushed, and pulled these children futilely to try to make them successful. In desperation, these parents even abandoned their children to their fates in hopes that John and Alice would finally learn how to succeed.

John, Alice, and the Talk Show Host were defeated in life not by the lack of proper skills, but by the difficulties they carried with them. The parents failed to help their children because the parents did not understand the true nature of the problem that overwhelmed their children.

In John, failure was caused by the way he transferred responsibility for himself to others in his life and by serious and debilitating dependencies on others, hidden by social charm and masked by manipulation. Alice had another problem. She initially did well in school motivated entirely to please her parents. As she grew older, she never outgrew the dominate motivation to please. As pleasing her parents with grades became increasingly difficult for her, a secret inadequacy and sense of isolation took root. Finally, to assuage her hidden pain, she turned her ambition and need for approval from her parents to her peers. Her underachievement, her deceptions, and her self-defeating behavior were driven by high ideals and a desperate need for self-esteem derived from gaining the approval of others. The Talk Show Host's underachievement partially evolved out of a childhood need for a closer emotional relationship with his aloof father and the Host's self-defeating perfectionism masked by disorganization and by his inability to sacrifice for what he truly wanted in his life.

As parents, if you do not understand chronic underachievement and what causes it in your child, then your techniques for motivation, study, and success will inevitably fail to help. What you do to help may even make things worse. If you wish to be effective, then your first task lies in understanding. You must understand the nature of underachievement and failure, why these problems exist, and what causes them in general terms and especially specifically in your child. Once you understand what causes these problems, then you can engage in a process of change that will have a better chance of success.

Let us concentrate on the first step—understanding.

Chapter 2

Characteristics of Underachievers

What I am going to do in the next few chapters is move from the surface of the problem down to its core in preparation for the later material on changing these patterns. Over the years, it has become evident to me that until parents identify and really understand the causes of their children's underachievement, creating positive change is difficult, if not impossible. Once you understand underachievement and what causes it, then you will understand why some of the usual things done to help will not work and why you would be better off following the program outlined later in this book.

The first level of understanding is a description of general characteristics of underachievers. The second level of understanding involves the character skills underachievers have failed to develop. Finally, the third level will lie in understanding the six different kinds of motivational patterns typical of most common forms of underachievement. The first level of discussion covers the general characteristics of all underachievers.

General Characteristics

Underachievers are bright: they don't put out effort necessary for success.

Underachievers typically demonstrate their intelligence on intelligence tests or on standardized achievement tests. On these instruments, they often score average or better, grade level or above. Teachers describe underachievers as having the tools, skills, and intelligence to do the required work. There are no physiological or neurological handicaps that by themselves significantly interfere with these children's capacities for success in class.

However, the necessary effort to master classroom material is erratic or poor. They may start out the year like a ball of fire, only to fade in the stretch. Grades may yo-yo from As to Fs throughout grading periods, or students may just get by through last-ditch efforts at the end of the school year. Scores on class tests may be very good, reflecting the students' learning, but homework, daily assignments, and long-term projects may be missing or late, resulting in significantly lower grades. Some underachievers actually study the wrong things for tests, refuse to study enough, or even not study at all just when critical effort is required.

The inconsistency or lack of effort is an enduring, recurring problem no matter what form it takes. Over time, some students become so discouraged that they give up altogether and daydream or sleep in class, skip class, or even refuse to go to school. Failure, underachievement, and the resulting discouragement originate in a lack of effort not in a lack of intelligence.

Underachievers lack persistence even when they want to do well.

The paradox of underachievement is that bright kids fail even when they want to do well. They fail not from a lack of desire, but from a failure to persist in the pursuit of their desires.

After ten years of service to hundreds of families seeking help for underachievement, I have learned that the vast majority of underachievers have internalized their parents' success values and want to do better. No matter what façade they present to their parents, no matter what act they put on to hide their true feelings, most students with consistently poor grades often envy good students and are ashamed of their poor performance. There are certainly those children who are so damaged by their family circumstances that success in class is completely rejected due to an absence or severe restriction in the proper values needed to sustain effort over time. These are not the majority, however. The kids I am talking about desire better things and possess the underlying values to help them work steadily, but they cannot manage to live out their values in real life. I know parents often complain about their children's broken promises to do better, yet, it is essential to understand that these children's promises are usually quite sincere at the time. The failure to persist in pursuit of desires and values is the real ailment. Lack of persistence dogs the lives of all underachievers.

Underachievement is a chronic problem and will not just go away by itself.

When a problem has persisted for over a year, then it has become a chronic problem, not a transient difficulty that will go away by itself. Temporary underachievement may occur for many reasons. Some children may become distracted by intense but disappointing peer relationships or family problems, and grades may temporarily fall. Achievers overcome these setbacks through increased effort toward independence and task mastery. Underachievers do not display increased independence and effort, but decreases in both. For example, children make transitions from one school to another, such as from grade school to middle school, or from junior high to high school. During these transitions, good students' grades may fall as they adjust to higher demands. Rarely do these adjustment periods last longer than a grading period or two because achievers readjust effort to match demands. Chronic underachievement may first emerge during these transitions, too. However, it does not go away. Independent effort does not increase to meet increased demands. Usually, it is the parents who must increase their efforts to motivate their children to work, not vice versa!

In my experience, underachievers do not simply outgrow their problems. Over the last ten years, whenever I have spoken to an audience about these difficulties, usually several parents approach me afterward to tell me about someone in their family who never outgrew underachievement. Sometimes, those parents confess that they themselves have been and still are underachievers. There are those individuals who have struggled and gotten better over time. Some of these may even have finally overcome their problems. But these are the minority, the exceptions that prove the rule.

Underachievement usually occurs in more than one area of life.

Parents with whom I have worked are most concerned about significant underachievement in school because poor grades close doors to their children's futures. The problem for most poorly motivated students is that their lack of effort and lack of success may not be confined only to school. Underachievers sabotage their success in almost any area where they have to work to develop talent to their potential. It is as though they get close to success and then back down. Many young men and women brought to my clinic by their parents have good athletic ability or musical talents. They may work hard for a while and achieve success and recognition, only to lose interest and motivation just when further work would prove most fruitful.

I interviewed one young man who had some success in two sports and in the school band only to quit each activity after achieving his first recognition. I have talked to coaches who have lamented the talent of an underachiever with a common complaint: "If he would only work at it he could be the best on the team." I have heard similar complaints from employers with whom I have consulted about their underachieving employees. Tragically, underachievement is often a pervasive pattern of maladaptive living and poor motivation. It is a lifestyle of backing down from challenge, self-defeat, and broken hopes that recur across many different situations and life circumstances. It is a tough way to try to live.

Underachievers do not do ordinary tasks.

Ironically, most situations in which underachievement occurs do not involve the accomplishment of extraordinary objectives or goals. Underachievers never (or rarely) stretch their abilities to the limits. Rather, underachievers fail at doing the mundane, ordinary tasks that lead to success. Achieving students may take demanding courses and not do well because the work is above their ability level. Achievers still learn and still try hard. Underachievers may be the ones who could make the honor roll, but make Cs and Ds in average level classes, not because the class demands are beyond their abilities, but because they failed to do the ordinary tasks that make achievement possible. Underachievers fail at performing adequately on tasks that are within their reach.

Character Problems

The second level of understanding underachievers involves their difficulties in character development. Most underachievers are good kids in that they have internalized the core values and ideals learned from their parents that would make sustained achievement possible. However, there are certain primary skills that over time and with practice become part of an individual's personality, or character, and if missing or underdeveloped, the individual will not be able to actualize his ideals or values in the real world. This is the fate from which most underachievers suffer. They have the intelligence, they have the desire, but they lack the character-based skills it takes to make their desires and intelligence work to bring them success and self-esteem.

Most laypeople who try to help underachievers overcome their problems approach these kids from a very misguided direction. They assume that underachievers have problems with organizational skills, study habits, time management difficulties, or deficiencies in academic learning that cause them to have poor grades. Therefore, underachievers are given study skills and organizational training or they are sent to tutors. These kinds of skills are secondary to character development, and as such, these strategies are almost always a waste of time because the skills underachievers lack are much more fundamental than these rather easily learned habits. The skills lacked are discussed below.

Underachievers lack self-discipline.

A life without self-discipline is not worth living because nothing of note can be accomplished without it. There are two types of self-discipline that piggyback on each other. Without one type, the other cannot exist for long. One is the discipline of getting started, and the other is the discipline of commitment to the task at hand. Without either, sustained success is impossible.

The first type of self-discipline gets one started on tasks when one does not feel like doing it. Self-discipline is not needed to start a task when one wants to work, but only when one is not inspired or in the proper mood. If one only starts tasks when one feels like it or when the mood strikes, then achievement will be sporadic, at best. It takes no self-discipline to talk on the phone, hang out with friends, watch television, or play games. But what happens when it is time to begin work and one does not want to work? If one is an achiever, then one sits down to start work even when one does not feel like it. Starting work is independent of mood, but is dependent, instead on one's goals and one's plans to meet those goals. Underachievers rarely practice self-discipline, and so most often, discipline to start work depends on others.

A self-disciplined individual knows that feelings of the moment are not the best basis for making many decisions in life. The future is also a basis for decisions. For example, a student needs to start writing a paper for an English class. He knows that if he does not allow enough time, the consequences will likely not be favorable, such as making a poor grade. When the time comes to start the paper, he may not actually feel like working, but he also is aware of the bad consequences of procrastination on future achievement, and he is also aware of the positive feelings aroused by success. Because he is aware of both the present feelings and the likely feelings in the future, a self-disciplined individual makes himself sit down, take pencil in hand, and start his writing task. Negative feelings of the moment do not control his behavior, rather, future goals do. An underachiever who is without self-discipline literally will not consider the future consequences of his actions. If he does not want to start for the moment, he obeys his present feelings and does something other than begin his task. One act of procrastination leads to another until the work is either not done, done late, or done poorly. Underachievers do not direct behavior toward future goals, but to the pleasures and escapes of the moment.

Commitment to the task is another form of self-discipline underachievers often lack. Commitment is a form of self-discipline that helps maintain persistence to task completion when fatigue or other negative factors interfere with performance. Commitment demands more from an individual than just starting a job. Commitment to a task is an emotional obligation to complete a task in a caring way, so that the task is done well. This form of self-discipline leads one to care about one's work, even when initial feelings toward the work are negative.

Both of these two forms of self-discipline, starting and caring, require that one develops an attitude of submission to living completely in the moment at hand and surrender to one's own values. For example, the "moment at hand" is an upcoming exam in biology. "Doing one's best" is a value defined by mastering the biology material at an A level for the exam. Now, commitment to completion of this task is to study and learn the material at a high level of mastery, so the student develops ways to test himself as to whether he knows the material well enough or not. Commitment is to keep studying the body of material until it is mastered. All study behavior occurs in a moment in time. To live that moment fully, a student would not let himself off the hook. He would be constantly aware of his goal, what material he did not understand or know. He would feel some anxiety about doing well, and would use that anxiety to keep himself alert and learning, and he would try to pace his learning to reach his goal. Every time he was tempted to quit before he had actually mastered the material, he would face that temptation with a renewed sense of obligation, whether that meant seeking help, taking a temporary break or rest from studying, or making himself continue to study. His work or studying would reflect this submission to both the task and to his values about caring and doing well. The more he committed to completing the task and to caring about it, the more intense his interest and richer his life would become because he could live each moment completely committed. This is the essence of goal-directed, self-disciplined behavior.

It is ironic that underachievers, most of whom seem only to want a good time, suffer often from either boredom and emptiness or from the sense of inadequacy and depression that results from trying to escape from those feelings of commitment, value, and self-discipline. They are bored and empty because they cannot submit to the here and now. They do not live the moment to its fullest and involve themselves in life's daily demands.

The voice of conscience exists in underachievers; they are good kids. When confronted with failure, they may promise to do better next time, and such promises reflect their true feelings of remorse. They value success and have internalized the value of "doing your best" in school. However, they do not listen to the small voice of conscience, that authority within, when it whispers to them. They may hear it: "Don't quit, work harder, keep going." However, they do not submit to that voice within them, to their own values in the living moment. Instead, they ignore it and do something else.

This lack of submission to the task and to their values is

not a form of rebellion. It is a form of denial. At least rebellion would replace one value with another one. Underachievers do not submit, but they do not develop new values, either. They complete few long-term goals and fail their promise, not because they develop new goals and values, but because they fail to commit to almost anything that requires long-term commitments and self-discipline. This lack of submission to the values of task completion and to caring leads them to have empty, meaningless lives, wasted in mindless pseudo-rebellion from their own conscience and the values of their parents. Ultimately, their failure of submission is a failure to seize freedom and control over their own destiny. Without self-discipline, failure and emptiness in life are almost assured.

Underachievers fail to accept responsibility for themselves.

Underachievers do not accept responsibility for themselves. They almost always blame everyone else or things beyond their control for their lack of effort and follow-through on work. If a class or a teacher is boring, then it is up to others to take care of those feelings for him because he cannot contain negative feelings and get work done. In fact, almost all underachievers fail to assume command of their own emotional states, positive or negative, and those aspects of the self that are connected to emotions, such as motivation, are forever outside their command. They never learn to develop and sustain their own motivation because they never learn to develop and sustain their own feelings.

Underachievers do not sacrifice for the future.

Underachievers have life backward. They sacrifice long-term goals for short-term pleasures. All sustained success requires sacrifice of something else. There is a great reward and sense of deep joy that arises from having to give a project everything one's got to reach a desired end. Every step of the way along the path to success one must make decisions to put off some pleasures for the future. Achievers often learn how to experience joy or pleasure in the work it takes to create long-term success, so that all along the way, the achiever is feeling the pleasures of hard work and the accomplishment of goals. The underachiever has little faith in work and, in fact, may hate it. He therefore connects negative feelings to doing the work it takes to create long-term success. In the face of negative feelings aroused when they must work, it often becomes easier and easier for them to think of a multitude of things they would rather do than do homework or study for exams. Hate, anger, boredom, and resentments accumulate and become barriers to success. Most underachievers cannot even imagine feeling positive emotions about work and study in school. Eventually, their own negative feelings overwhelm their rational behavior. They underachieve once more.

Underachievers are dependent in their work.

Underachievers are dependent in their efforts and have to be supervised to do their work. They may have spurts of time where they work independently, but when left to themselves, they cannot sustain independence. They work best over time when they are supervised or when given one-on-one instruction.

Dependent functioning occurs when underachievers fail to regulate their own behavior to meet ordinary expectations. They must be reminded to prepare for tests, bring books home, and take materials to school. Teachers must supervise classroom behavior so the child will work or not disrupt class. Dependency also exists when parents or other adults must constantly enforce or set limits on a child when the child knows full well what the limits are . . . he just refuses to set limits on himself. Examples of this are when a child comes home late for curfew, disrupts siblings' activities, interrupts conversations of others, clowns inappropriately in class, fails to regulate anger, and is a source of disharmony in the home or school. Their dependency sends a message that if they are not carefully watched and monitored, they will do something irresponsible to sabotage themselves.

Dependency means that underachievers force others to make decisions for and about them, thus avoiding having to become responsible for themselves. Being disorganized, missing deadlines, procrastinating, and dawdling force someone else to take charge and decide what must be done: whether that's extending deadlines or punishing the tardiness. Chronically missing deadlines and procrastination also invites more supervision, which further fuels inappropriate dependency on others. Underachievers are often masters at making other people take care of them.

Dependent functioning also occurs at the emotional level, when underachievers refuse to experience appropriate worry and anxiety in their lives. By being late, by failing to do ordinary things, underachievers cause their parents (and others) to worry excessively about them. The fact that others worry about them secretly makes dependent individuals feel more secure, even though they may be unaware that their security is tied to making others worry about them. The fact that adolescent underachievers often complain that their parents constantly bug them does not change the fact at all that their behavior consistently garners their parents' overinvolvement and worry.

When a parent or teacher worries about an underachiever, the parent or teacher becomes increasingly emotionally involved with that child. Underachievers respond viscerally to such anxieties in others. They feel reassured that they will be taken care of and not be abandoned to function in life on their own. Making others worry about them is one way underachievers connect their umbilical cords firmly to the emotions of others and thus free themselves from anxiety and worry.

Individuals who are not worried about what the major factors of life, such as their future education—or the lack of it—will bring them, are secretly dependent on others to do their worrying for them. The essence of dependence is to have a worry-free life. The essence of responsibility is the reverse of dependency: it is to feel anxiety and to feel the pain of worrying about things. Healthy individuals will experience their own anxieties and then work realistically to take care of their worries, thus feeling better. They work to take care of problems. People who do not worry do not work. Underachievers will refuse to experience anxiety and will not work to take care of problems. The long-term results of such a dependent lifestyle are to experience increasing despair and emptiness when their lives lose meaning. They can also become enraged at successful people who refuse to take care of them and feed their inordinate demands for entitled dependency.

Dependency extends deeper into the character of a child to the processes of thinking itself. Underachievers do not even engage in the process of thinking productively about solving their problems. When asked how they will get the grades they may want or achieve their desires, they often respond with variants of the ubiquitous, "I don't know." Underachievers wait for others to create possible solutions for them to follow, and then they fail to follow through on those solutions.

Underachievers fear feelings of personal responsibility.

Whenever I am counseling with parents to help them understand their underachieving children, I often have to work hard to get them to understand this one essential problem almost all underachievers have: the fear of increased responsibility that comes with success.

Quite often, especially when the parents have sustained successes in their lives, they forget how much anxiety they felt when they first began to assume responsibility for themselves as youths. Successful parents and achieving teenagers see challenges in a personal way, as an opportunity to explore their potential, to reach new heights, as a chance to feel good and proud of themselves. To individuals with such an attitude, the feeling of being responsible for success or failure is a feeling of empowerment they relish. No so for underachievers. Underachievers see challenges and the personal responsibility as threats. Their emotional response to that threat is fear, and they inevitably back down from challenge and avoid the feeling of threat by remaining irresponsible. By avoiding challenge, underachievers never learn how to connect positive feelings of satisfaction and excitement to challenges, but, instead, experience only negative emotions.

Every success leads to new problems to solve. For example, if an underachiever finally makes himself sit down at a specified time to study for a math test, he must now actually get his math book out and learn the material. If he is successful today, then he will have to be successful again tomorrow. What if he cannot do it again? When underachievers do experience a run of successes, teachers and parents who are praising them are often unaware that underneath, underachievers are not feeling good, but are experiencing increases in anxiety and other negative feelings. These negative emotions are attached to effort and success. To gain a sense of equilibrium, underachievers unconsciously arrange failure for themselves again by irresponsible behavior. This way, underachievers avoid all the new problems sustained success brings them. They can live in the old, familiar, painful, but secure ways of continuing underachievement.

Underachievers make excuses that keep them irresponsible.

Part of growing up is learning to be honest with oneself and accept appropriate responsibility when one has made mistakes. When children learn to be honest with themselves and others, they gradually learn to assume control over themselves and, bit by bit, grow more like adults as they mature. If children refuse to assert responsibility for themselves, they will not mature, but will cling to childhood patterns of emotion and dependency.

Excuses help children cope temporarily with feelings of pressure, guilt, or anxiety. The excuses of children carry the message, "I didn't just do something I obviously did (denial of reality)," or "It's not my fault." Excuses keep feelings of responsibility at bay and retard insight and maturity. If children cling to excuses too fervently and too long, the children in effect cling to childish ways of coping with reality. They run the danger of never developing successful ways of coping with pressures and the normal anxieties of growing up. In fact, underachievers tend to turn excuse-making into a lifestyle and an art form.

Excuses are probably universal in young children, and are actually helpful for a while. However, underachievers cling to their excuses long after it is developmentally appropriate for them to do so. They doggedly commit themselves to maintaining excuses and fail to create effective action to solve problems.

Underachievers make excuses for almost every failure or shortcoming. The excuses range from the flimsy to the profound, such as "The class is boring," "I forgot," "The teacher didn't tell us about the test," "The teacher doesn't like me," or, my favorite excuse for failure, "I don't know." I have even heard kids tell such long, involved excuses for why they failed to do something that in order to make sense of the excuse, parents have almost had to create charts and graphs to follow the twisting paths and side streets of excuse after excuse for a significant failure.

Excuses perniciously destroy children's self-esteem and confidence by robbing them of a sense of control and power over their own lives and making them feel inwardly helpless. Excuses send a message to parents and teachers that they (the children) are not able to change, because nothing is their fault. The underachiever's excuses mean: "I'm not in charge; therefore, I can do nothing to help myself. I am defeated by forces and circumstances outside or inside myself over which I have no power or influence." These forces are experienced as over-whelming. It is as though children are saying, "I do not create my problems and I can do nothing to prevent their occurrence, reduce their influence, or change myself to cope successfully with them. I am simply a victim, and therefore, life is unfair."

There are two major kinds of excuses. These are external and internal excuses. Understanding these two kinds of excuses will prove helpful in later chapters in creating strategies to get rid of them.

External excuses blame other people and external circum-stances for the individual's own problems. For example, when asked why they do not do well in a class, many underachievers complain that the class (or teacher or textbooks, or almost everything else) is boring. What underachievers want is for their parents to buy these excuses and quit asking questions. If par-ents do, the underachievers have successfully convinced their unwary parents that they are not responsible for their own interest levels, but that teachers should be more entertaining, or books more interestingly written. These children are now off the hook for their poor grades and lack of effort, and more importantly for development of good character, they are off the hook for controlling their own feelings. Further, in order to convince parents, children must also convince themselves of the validity of these excuses. When children do convince themselves, they destroy their chance of self-esteem. Any excuse that blames external circumstances for failure to study, turn in homework, produce effort, or perform adequately in class falls in this category of an external excuse.

Internal excuses blame something in the children that is permanent and cannot change; therefore, they still are not responsible for themselves and their efforts at learning. For example, when they are asked to account for why they did not study for an important test, leave important books or homework at school, or failed to listen in class, they may use the excuse, "I forgot." They act like memory problems are inner defects over which they have no control whatsoever. Someone else must be their memory for them, and usually, this someone else is a parent, a teacher, or some combination of a more responsible adult. Sometimes, parents hand their children excuses on a silver platter. I recall one young man who told his father, "Dad, you're right. I'm just lazy. I guess I was born that way, so you're going to have to get used to my bad grades, because I can't change the way I was born."

Both external and internal excuses hide a fundamental truth. Underachievers make decisions that inexorably lead them to fail. One sophomore came home from school and put down his books on the kitchen table. He ate something. After finishing his snack, he remembered an important English assignment due the next day. Instead of getting to work on it after recalling the assignment, he watched television. One thing led to another, and he did not do his assignment. He told me the following day he had "forgotten" all about his English assignment. The sad fact is that he did not forget it at all. When he remembered his assignment, he *chose* to watch television. His excuse, "I forgot," got him off the hook from being responsible for making a choice. In fact, the excuse even allowed him to escape the fact that he had even made a decision to begin with.

Underachievement is a choice kids make, but one which they do not know they are making. Their excuses keep them blind, deaf, and dumb to their choices, and keep them ignorant of how to make different choices in the future. As long as excuses remain intact and unchallenged, these children will be unable to change.

Underachievers lie to themselves and others.

A child comes home from school. One of the first things his mother asks him when they meet is, "Do you have any homework?" He says, "No, I did it at school." She wonders, "Is he lying?" In this very moment, the tensions and negative feelings in the family are revealed because lying is almost a daily occurrence in the home during the school year.

For parents, lying is an insidious and disheartening aspect of underachievement. Their children lie to them constantly about school. Parents never know when to believe their children because lying tears at the very fabric of trust that bonds parents and their children together.

Good parents who rear underachievers are constantly torn between two opposing feelings. On the one hand, their hearts tell them to trust their children because they believe their children are good, because they love them, and because they want to believe in them fully. On the other hand, their judgment and experience tells them that when it comes to school, their children twist and mold the truth to hide themselves and their behavior from their parents. They lie despite the parents' values and the children's own long-term welfare.

Sometimes underachievers lie so well it is scary. At times, I have to remind myself that these kids do have a conscience, even if it is sometimes very hard to find evidence of it.

What most parents do not understand is that lying also sends a dependency message. The lies say to parents, "If you really want to know the truth about me, then you have to become so involved and entangled in my life that I will never have to be separated from you." In fact, the message is that parents will have to become master detectives and check up on their children at almost every turn to make sure they know what is really going on.

More importantly, beyond the ascertainment of facts about school, the psychology of lying goes even deeper. Underachievers constantly send the message that something basic is wrong with the way they approach life. By lying about the facts of school life, they are also lying about what is really wrong inside of them. Lying about externals, such as homework and grades, focuses parents' attention on the wrong things, while the problems that cause the lying to begin with often remain untouched and unexplored inside the children who lie. How is it that normally good children who have internalized a good conscience can cut themselves off from their values and seemingly violate those values so easily and not suffer guilt or shame when they do? Why do their consciences not work to make them feel so badly when they lie that they will stop lying and tell the truth for once?

Actually, most underachievers do have a conscience that operates rather well. Chronic lying enables underachievers to sever ties with their own deeply held values and avoid openly feeling the guilt and shame that come when they violate themselves. The engines of conscience continue to grind away at their self-esteem and leave them feeling inadequate, inferior, and ill at ease. Instead of facing themselves openly, however, they hide in the lies. If parents focus only on the facts their children lie about and never on the deeper psychology of lying, then parents simply feed the problem even more. They help their children avoid the painful feelings created by a conscience robbed of its power by lies, by excuses, and by dependency. It is the unacknowledged conscience that grinds away at self-esteem, self-confidence, self-motivation, and achievement. The engines of conscience drive the children into discouragement and continued failures. Until they overcome lying, underachievers remain self-defeating children.

Underachievers lack self-mastery.

Self-mastery, as I mean it, involves the ability to influence emotional states through behavior and thought. To some extent, people control their typical emotional reactions to life around them by their usual attitudes and ways of seeing things. For example, if I believe people are saying mean things about me behind my back, I may feel angry and hurt over rejections even if other people are not rejecting me or saying mean things about me. My beliefs control my emotions and influence my behavior, even if my beliefs are erroneous. Self-mastery is both the awareness that I control many of my own emotions and a willingness to exert conscious control over my attitudes and emotions.

Underachievers do not see themselves as having much control over their own thoughts, emotions, or feelings. For instance, if underachievers feel bored with history, then it is "history's" fault or the teacher's responsibility to entertain them so they will bother to learn history. To underachievers, it is not up to them to involve themselves in a class, to learn new material, or to find learning satisfying. These children habitually blame others or circumstances beyond their control for their failures and lack of learning. Severe underachievers are often so hostile to schoolwork and success that they suffer low self-esteem, even depression, as a result of their failure to learn to master their own feelings. Once these children turn off to success and learning, it is very difficult to reach them through educational means alone. Anger and discouragement may become chronic conditions for these children and for their parents and teachers who try to help them.

It is interesting to talk to highly achieving students about the issue of self-mastery and schoolwork. One sixteen-year-old high school junior was a straight-A student in an advanced honors program in her school. At report card time, I overheard a conversation she had with some of her friends on my front porch as she was getting ready to baby-sit my two younger daughters. Her friends were complaining about their grades. When the conversation drifted around to her, she told her friends that she had made no grades below a 95 (A) in her honors classes, consisting of calculus, chemistry, French, English, and history. When the other girls exclaimed how she must be a brain, she remained calm. She asked them what they did on Friday afternoon after school. They usually played around. She told them she studied until around six o'clock in the evening before going out with her boyfriend. She also told them she studied ahead every weekend on Saturday mornings and Sunday afternoons. She also worked part-time and was saving money to buy her own car. When the other girls asked her why she worked so hard, she told them she did not want her parents to have to pay for her college, that she wanted to get an academic scholarship to any university in the country. Her friends seemed a little awed by the girl. Apparently they did not know she did so well in school. "You seem so normal," one girl actually said. "You must love homework." At this point, the honor student seemed to lose a little patience. "Look, I'm just like you," she said. "When I get home from school, many times I'm sick of it, and I don't want to do my homework either. Sometimes I'd rather do almost anything but study. But every night I sit down to it, and once I get started, I get involved and it's not so bad then. In fact, I feel really good about my work, and I'm proud of my grades. Sometimes it's boring, but so what? I still have to do it if I'm going to get what I want."

This honor student had learned to master her attitudes, behavior, and emotions. She was able to change boredom and disinterest into involvement and interest in learning. She was able to change her feelings because she made herself work toward goals she had set for herself. If at times she was still bored with schoolwork, she had the maturity and presence of mind to contain negative feelings and get her work done anyway. She was willing to work for her pride.

Roadblocks inevitably arise to frustrate the pursuit of goals.

Individuals who have learned to master their own feelings can master their frustration and not let frustration control their feelings about themselves and their goals. In fact, changing negative feelings into positive ones during the process of attaining goals is crucial for sustaining motivation for success.

Underachievers invariably have difficulty changing negative feelings into positive ones, or even in believing that such a change is possible or even desirable. Over and over again, the experience in my clinic is that underachievers can be led to start working harder, but stubbornly and persistently cling to negative feelings about what they are doing.

Once underachievers start working at school tasks, I typically ask if they would like to feel better about doing their work? Astoundingly, the answer I get most of the time is "No." Literally, they just want to get their work done and continue to hate it.

The notion that they can take the ultimate responsibility for themselves and actually change the way they feel about something without necessarily changing the "something" itself unsettles or even frightens most underachievers. They would rather cling to childhood negativity.

Unfortunately, continuing to connect negative feelings to work makes it quite difficult to sustain work. Even when success is sustained through negative feelings by the sheer force of will, such success will have a pleasureless, driven quality that robs individuals of one of the benefits of success: enhanced self-esteem and relaxed self-assurance. Under such circumstances, developing disciplined, motivated individuals who can enjoy achievement will be difficult, if not impossible, in most cases.

The growth of self-mastery in children and adolescents is

crucial if they are to sustain independent effort in stressful situations such as school. The children who can master their own feelings and behavior can change boredom into interest, anxiety into excitement, ignorance into knowledge, discouragement into encouragement, and shame and guilt into pride and accomplishment. The skill of self-mastery allows children to gain self-control, which enhances self-esteem and confidence that can only come from children who have grown increasingly certain that they can transform bad to good in their lives though their own efforts.

Underachievers lack insight and self-knowledge.

It is almost impossible to underestimate the role of self-ignorance in making sustained underachievement possible with any given youngster. Over and over again in my experience, underachievers lack a great deal of valuable information about themselves: their values, feelings, motivations, conflicts, and awareness of consistent self-defeating behavior. This ignorance causes pain and discourages them. They do not know why they fail, and they may not even know what or how they went about setting up failure. It is as though they have no clue as to what is going on within them.

One fifth grader finished a project on the theater at home. He secured an old shoe box and cut out cardboard figures to create a stage. His work was quite good, and he did it all by himself. However, the parents of this young man received a progress report in the mail, which indicated that he had a zero on the very project he had so creatively completed. The mother went to school to discuss things with the teacher. After explaining to the teacher how her son had completed his project, the teacher told her he had never turned it in. Upon a hunch, the teacher checked the young man's desk. There was the project hidden safely away. When asked about this theater project, the boy replied that he did not know why he did not turn it in. "I forgot" was his only answer.

"I forgot," "I don't know," and more subtly, telling parents what they want to hear but not the truth, are typical answers underachievers give to questions that require self-reflection and insight in order to answer honestly reasonable inquires about their own behavior.

Parents may mistakenly believe answers such as "I don't know," are evasive. However, many chronic underachievers really do not know what motivates them. They do not want to find out, either. Knowing oneself is the next of kin to becoming responsible for oneself, and underachievers fear and avoid accepting responsibility.

The fifth grader discussed above was in treatment with me at my clinic. At first, information about his behavior was not available to him to even begin to understand how he made decisions that led to failure. In such cases, I have learned it is best to take kids through a "sequence analysis" of their behavior. A "sequence analysis" is simply asking a youngster good questions about what happened, like the reconstruction of a story, from the beginning of a failure, through the middle, to the very end. In this case I asked him to tell me how he did the project, where in the house, and when he finished it. I asked him to tell me what he did next at home after he finished the project, where he put it for school the next day. In this painstaking way, step by step, I had him reconstruct the sequence of events that led up to the failure to turn it in, including in detail what he did in the classroom and what he was aware of as he was doing it.

Briefly, this young man was able to recall entering the classroom with his project in hand. However, as he looked around him at the other kids and their projects, he discovered his theater was not like theirs. All the other kids had colored in a theater stage, either on flat sheets of paper or in an old shoe box like his. His was the only one that had figures and stage pieces actually cut out and glued in place in a three-dimensional display. By having the child recall things in such rich detail, he was able to also report what he was thinking when he saw his project was so different from the others. He said, "I thought I had done mine wrong and the other kids would laugh at it." For this reason, he hid his project to avoid social disapproval and embarrassment.

Through this procedure of asking good "How did it happen?" questions, the child was able to discover two very important things about himself that he had lacked beforehand. The first thing he discovered of crucial importance was that he had not just "forgotten" to turn it in as he had half-believed before, but had actually made a decision to hide the project. He became aware he could have made another decision and not gotten a zero. Further, he became aware of a specific thought and motivation that influenced his failure: he was so in need of the approval of others that he would sacrifice success to avoid the shame of negative social evaluation. It was as though he was saying, "I'd rather fail in school than take a chance on being embarrassed."

The situation of the fifth grader is typical of underachievers of all ages. They do not know themselves. They do not see that they make decisions that arrange failure for themselves. Since they are ignorant of their decisions, they have nothing by which they can change their underachievement patterns. Secondly, they do not reflect on their actions, feelings, and thoughts to discover why they fail, so they remain a mystery to themselves as well as to others who care for them. Finally, without awareness of decisions and motivations, underachievers are never conscious of value conflicts within themselves that they must in some way resolve in order to achieve a self-directed purpose. They do not know who they are or what they are going to stand for in their lives.

The fifth grader above is a wonderful example of this latter failure of character. This was a young man who wanted to do well in school and would invariably feel bad about his failures. He had internalized success values from his parents. However, success values were in conflict with the high value he placed on peer acceptance and avoidance of social ostracism. In essence, he found the opinions of others to be more critical to his behavior than his desire to be successful. Ironically, this young man was so afraid of disapproval and rejection that he rarely knew the real opinions of others. He relied almost solely on his inner fantasies about what those opinions might be, and then reacted fearfully to the opinions he thought others might have about him. Rarely, if ever, did he actually test out his fears to see if they were true, and so he was able to save himself from having to cope with real rejection and disapproval by avoiding imagined rejection and disapproval. He lived a vicarious life that prevented him from learning from his experiences. In fact, the way he lived prevented him from having experiences that would challenge his fears directly. In truth, his need for approval conflicted with his need for achievement. Being totally unaware of his conflict with himself meant that he could not begin to take charge of his life and was chronically under-achieving.

The conflict in this particular child can be found in many other underachievers as well. If he, like many others, can avoid learning about such internal conflicts of conscience, then he, like others, will never finally have to resolve such conflicts through decisions and commitments to values. Without such self-knowledge, underachievers will not be able to exert some control over their own destinies. Rather, they will lead desperate lives and never understand why.

Chapter 3

Core Problems in Identity

Whenever I am conducting a seminar on discouraged children, I find that parents generally understand the kinds of issues I have discussed in the previous chapter. They see the lack of effort and the poor grades. They understand the problem is chronic and will not likely go away on its own. They even see how the characteristics of underachievers fit their children. They seem to understand all these things, but they still do not grasp the big picture until they understand that their children are not lacking in the area of motivation. As a matter of fact, until parents understand that their children are highly motivated individuals, they will generally fail to do what is necessary to help their children overcome underachievement and learn to succeed.

The crucial truth parents must grasp is that their underachieving children are highly motivated to do exactly what they do: fail. It is not that these kids openly seek out failure. Far from it. Rather, they are driven by motivations that either block them from being successful or that are incompatible with sustained effort toward success. The consistent result of these motivations is that they underachieve or even fail in school.

The motivations that block sustained success are unconscious. That is, underachievers lack insight into their own intentions, motivations, and choices to arrange failure for themselves in school. These youngsters are self-defeating, and they have no clue as to how or why they are not doing well. Even more, they are highly motivated to avoid finding out about their emotional and motivational blocks to achievement. They substitute excuses and denials of responsibility for insight, self-knowledge, and effective action in life; thus they remain deaf, dumb, and blind to what is going on within them.

The motivations that block achievement and lead to chronic discouragement fall into patterns or types of underachievers. These motivational patterns are quite complex. They involve children's core beliefs about their place in their respective families, relationship patterns with parents and peers, relationships with authorities, the development of conscience, and the way these children handle basic emotions, such as anger, anxiety, shame and guilt, and fears of the future. In other words, these motivational patterns form the core identity or self-concept of underachievers. These patterns are the roots of their problems with success.

Underachievers find changing their ways to become more successful quite difficult because the motivational patterns that cause underachievement make up the core of these children's ideas about themselves. A self-concept is much like an airplane's design characteristics. When a test pilot flies outside the design envelope of an airplane to test its limits, anxiety and a feeling of danger mount quickly. The plane is shaky and hard to control. The pilot is scared because any minute the plane could shake apart. This is how the underachiever feels when he forces himself to perform outside the design envelope of his own sense of identity. He is scared and feels fragile and alone. It is always much safer to fly only within the boundaries already established for one's sense of self rather than to push oneself outside those boundaries. The difference between airplanes and underachievers is that people's sense of identity or "design envelope" can grow and change when people face the crossroads of their lives where the boundaries of self are pushed further out.

Facing the crossroads of one's identity is natural in the journey from childhood to adulthood. There are many crises of identity and many changes in identity as one grows up. Further, identity is not a unitary, monolithic thing. One may have many self-concepts that make up one's sense of self. Identity, in practical terms, may be thought of as a statement of "who I am." An identity or self-concept exists because an individual is able to draw psychological boundaries in life that define oneself in certain ways. One includes some things and excludes others in ones definition of oneself. Now, the greater the emotional commitment to a self definition, the longer one has had it, and the more emotions, thoughts, perceptions, values, attitudes, and behavioral habits are tied into a particular self-concept, then the more committed a person is to maintaining that self-concept or identity and the more difficult it is to change, even when one is highly motivated to make a change.

Early in my professional training I was involved in an experimental program using hypnosis to help people stop smoking. Candidates for the program were screened for their need and good motivation to quit smoking. Some people referred themselves for treatment; others were referred by their physicians. When the professional staff began to explore the results of the hypnosis programs to understand why the treatment worked for some people and not for others, we discovered the power of identity to either thwart positive change or help change occur.

Essentially, we found that almost all our patients in the beginning of treatment defined themselves as smokers. The ones for whom the smoking program failed to help still defined themselves as smokers several months later at the end of treatment. However, individuals who did quit smoking defined themselves quite differently. They defined themselves as nonsmokers. What we believed happened was this: People who still thought of themselves as smokers would use willpower and try to quit smoking. For a while, their efforts would make them successful, but they were always fighting against the grain of how they defined themselves. Whenever "smokers" felt a strong urge to light up a cigarette, they would fight the urge until their willpower gave out and they lit up. However, those who were able to redefine themselves as "nonsmokers" did not seem to exert much willpower whenever a strong urge to smoke came over them. They handled the urge to smoke like all the other nonsmokers of the world: They just let the urge pass and did not smoke.

What this experience in treating smoking habits taught me was the power of self-concept in human motivation. Trying only to change behavior without also changing one's self-concept makes behavior change quite fragile over time. The change in identity or self-concept seemed to me much more fundamental, indeed, necessary for changes in habits to become lasting.

Although achievement and underachievement involve much more complex behavior and attitudinal patterns than smoking or nonsmoking, the identity issues still rule the individual's destiny just as surely as identity ruled treatment outcome for the smokers who wanted to change. In an overly simple example, how does a youngster who defines himself as an A student handle a strong urge to goof off and not study for a test or do his homework one evening? He handles it by studying for his test and doing his work anyway and doing his tasks well (and usually feels proud of himself for fulfilling his identity). On the other hand, how does an underachiever handle the same strong urge to goof off and not work or study? By fulfilling his self-concept and not performing as required.

I have rarely encountered a child or adolescent who defines himself as an underachiever, per se. However, I have encountered many youngsters whose sense of identity involving school and achievement did not allow them to do well in school. Some kids have told me they are "bad" in math or in English. Sure enough, that is where they did their worst. Some kids with excellent potential have told me that they did not want to make good grades because others might think of them as "nerds." These kids' sense of identity ran counter to the demands of school and responsibility. More pervasively, other kids defined themselves as the "black sheep" of the family, the ones who always messed up, and they would find creative ways of fulfilling the destiny such an identity demanded they fulfill.

The examples of identity mentioned above are straightforward and relatively accessible to common sense. There are deeper layers to identity, more subtle and more powerful self-concept difficulties that are not so easily accessible, nor easily changed without evoking intense anxiety in the individual who undergoes the effort to change or sometimes in the parents as well.

Most underachievers require their parents' help to change. Understanding the identity patterns that underlie chronic underachievement is often crucial because as children begin to change, they will often reveal the previously hidden emotions, perceptions, and attitudes that cause their problems. If parents do not understand what is going on, they miss many opportunities to help their children gain important insights and learn how to change themselves. In addition, families have identity patterns just as the children do who spring from them. If change is ever to occur in the children, the parents must understand how they may have inadvertently contributed to their children's problems.

The next six chapters are devoted to sketching six types of motivation and behavior that make up common identity patterns of typical underachievers and their families. Most underachievers fall within these six types, and some children seem to have characteristics of more than one type. Usually, however, one of these six patterns forms the axis around which the destiny of a child unfolds as he rolls toward his future.

Chapter 4

The Procrastinator

Years ago, a friend of mine said there is good and bad procrastination. Good procrastination is when you have a lot to do and little time in which to do it. You set priorities by putting some tasks off until the last minute in order to do others. You set aside three hours to do a two-hour job. You procrastinate, but you get your work done. Bad procrastination is having things to do, but you never get around to doing them. So when the deadline approaches, you spend three minutes doing a two-hour job. As a consequence, the task is done poorly, if at all. The Procrastinator underachiever is a master of bad procrastination.

Putting things off until it is too late, dawdling, and wasting time, is more characteristic of the Procrastinator than almost any other type of underachiever, especially when it comes to doing tasks they do not wish to do. On such tasks, they typically give every indication they are willing to perform as asked, but never seem to get around to it. Something else comes up or they forget. They may complete their homework under parental

51

supervision at home, and may even do it quite well. However, the next day in class, they may not turn in the assignment for a variety of reasons.

A typical pattern for Procrastinators is something like this. They put off going to their locker to get their homework until it is too late to go to the locker if they want to get to class on time. They go to class and leave their homework behind. Then they complain to their exasperated teachers and parents that they did not have time to go to their locker before class. Somehow, one must presume it is the school's fault for not having lockers closer to class.

Procrastinators' excuses for failure tend to project an image of helplessness. It is as though things could not have turned out any differently. They act like victims of circumstances, misfortune, or the unfair demands and actions of others. They are full of good intentions that are somehow never fulfilled, usually through no fault of their own. When parents or teachers expect them to live up to their talents, these underachievers often whine and complain that unjustified demands are being made on their time and abilities.

Procrastinators are usually good kids who are liked by many of their peers and teachers. They rarely show tempers or other signs of anger directly. Often described as "sweet" or "nice" kids, they are rarely discipline problems in the classroom. However, their compliant attitudes and easygoing natures only serve to hide an iron-willed opposition to the demands placed on them at school and at home. At a teacher conference, parents of such a student will hear a teacher complain about their child, "He's such a nice boy, but he's so slow and forgetful about his work!"

When these students are confronted with their irresponsibility and punished, they usually get worse. Under pressure, they get sulky, irritable, or argumentative, and blame others for being unfair to them. In fact, confrontation usually serves only to increase their already considerable sense of discouragement and may make these youngsters depressed or even worsen their procrastination. In older adolescents, confrontation and exposure of their irresponsibility may provoke outright anger and rebellion in normally good-natured and compliant individuals. Usually Procrastinators rationalize their behavior. They feel entirely justified in not doing what is demanded of them because they feel nagged and unfairly criticized. They continue to passively oppose and resent demands made on them by dawdling and procrastinating, or by doing a careless job when they could have done a more careful one.

Procrastinators are masters at engaging others in endless power struggles, which they invariably win by passively forgetting to do an assigned task. They rarely outright refuse to do something demanded of them, they just never get around to it. Furthermore, these underachievers blame others for the frustration that inevitably results from such power struggles. These underachievers are consummate victims. They cunningly provoke others to feel frustrated, angry, and helpless, and then feel abused when others respond to them with anger.

For example, a father once demanded that his fourteen-year-old son mow the lawn by 5:30 P.M. Friday evening. Naturally, this young man put off the task all week until late Friday afternoon. He walked outside, saw a few dark clouds in the sky, and decided he could not mow the lawn since it might rain. When the father got home at 6:00 P.M. he found his son watching television and angrily confronted him. The son felt picked on and complained to his father, "You can't mow the lawn when it rains!" The father made his son immediately mow the lawn by threatening to punish him. Filled with resentment, the young man mowed the lawn as his father demanded. When he had finished, the father inspected the lawn and found little tufts of grass sticking up in several places in the yard. When the father confronted his son about the poorly done job, the young man blamed the "stupid" lawn mower and complained that sweat had gotten in his eyes so that he could not see well. Several hours later, the young man asked his mother, "Why is Dad always mad at me?"

Because they blame others or circumstances for their difficulties, Procrastinators have little insight into how they cause their own problems. Sometimes these underachievers have even been known to openly enjoy making others angry at them in order to justify their resistance to ordinary life tasks.

The problem behaviors of Procrastinators are more often those of omission rather than commission. These underachievers believe that they do not do anything offensive, and therefore, the negative reactions of others to them are unjustified and unfair. Consequently, they fail to take responsibility for how their actions negatively affect their own goals and the reactions of others to them. They complain how unfairly they are treated by teachers and parents, how siblings get by with doing less work than them, that their parents never listen to them or never let them do things they want, and how others always are picking on them. When reasonable courses of corrective action are suggested, these underachievers will "yes but" themselves to death, coming up with an endless variety of why good suggestions will not work in their cases. They rarely acknowledge their noncompliance. Rather, they escape responsibility for their failures by portraying problem situations as though they were due to accidents, misunderstandings, or the unreasonable behavior of others. These underachievers try the patience of the most mild mannered and forgiving individuals who have dealings with them. People who are in charge of these underachievers rarely escape the uncomfortable feeling that they have just been taken advantage of by these kids.

Causes

Procrastinators do not learn their behavior patterns from the neighbors. Sometimes, one or both parents have the same problems as their child. The child learns how to procrastinate and blame the world around him for his behavior by modeling the way the parents react to their circumstances.

If parents promise to do things to or for their children, but just never seem to get around to it, they are providing good models for children to learn to be good procrastinators. One or both parents may reveal a frequent tendency to "forget" obligations to their children or others in such a way that lets them off the hook for being responsible for their failures. For instance, they may fail to show up for therapy appointments to help their children overcome underachievement and justify it by saying, "It just slipped my mind." Sometimes parents even inadvertently provide the excuses that a child uses to avoid doing things asked of him. "Oh, he's just normal. All kids are like this," a mother may say to justify her child's procrastination. Parents may blame the teachers or the school and not focus on the child's problem behavior. An even more sophisticated way the parents put off doing something effective to help their child is expressed in the words of one father in referring to his son, "He'll be all right. He's just like me when I was his age. I didn't do well in school either." Parental procrastination in dealing with problem behaviors of their children not only provides a model for the children to follow in dealing responsibly with problems, but also provides training in rationalizing nonaction.

At the core of Procrastinators' motivational difficulties lies strongly held, self-defeating beliefs about anger and the expression of personal desires. Procrastinators generally have a strong taboo against telling other people how they feel about things and expressing hostility directly. The expression of desire or negative emotions is dangerous or threatening to them. They learn to express desires and negative feelings indirectly and expect other people to know what they want and to give it to them without having to ask for it. When Mom or Dad or teachers cannot read their minds, these children feel resentful and cheated. Procrastinators do more than just inhibit the open expression of their feelings. They actually hide their true feelings from others and even from themselves. However, they express anger or resentment indirectly by artfully and passively refusing to do what parents or teachers ask of them. They learn that such behavior is effective in getting revenge on parents and teachers for hurts, real or imagined. Their lack of insight into their anger, their taboos about openly expressing feelings, desires, and negative emotions, inevitably leads to their denial of angry feelings and personal desires, and an avoidance of open hostility, and a passivity in the face of challenging demands. Procrastinators have learned to express dissatisfaction and anger indirectly rather than through forthright and honest communication.

Parents of the Procrastinators may inadvertently teach their children indirect expression of disagreement with authority and other negative feelings. In a classic case of this type, a parent pledged to not wake up her child during the school week, but to allow her son to suffer the consequences of his own failure to get himself up on time. For two weeks she dutifully refused to awaken her son, and he got to school on time for the two weeks. However, the father sheepishly confessed his wife's strategy. She did not wake up her son, but when she left for work, she called her husband on the car phone to wake him up so that he could go upstairs and wake up their son. The mother had secretly objected to the idea of not waking up her son and letting him suffer the consequences on his own. She was dissatisfied with the treatment suggestion, but had chosen to remain silent and noncompliant. For those two weeks, his mother "forgot" her appointment at my office on two occasions so that she would avoid confronting her feelings openly. In such situations, children may learn to express their own dissatisfactions indirectly, also. When they become dissatisfied with school, they express their negative feelings indirectly through procrastination, passive noncompliance, dawdling, and forgetfulness. Poor grades and underachievement are the inevitable results of such indirect means of self-expression.

For Procrastinators, underachievement in school does not result from a conscious decision to mess up. Rather, poor grades result from their successful attempts to control and avoid the open expression of anger, resentment, dissatisfaction, or other negative feelings. Procrastination, forgetfulness, whining about the "impossible" expectations of others, and dawdling are merely symptoms that allow these children to escape knowing themselves and accepting responsibility for their actions, emotions, and conflicts. This is a very important point that most parents completely misunderstand about their children.

Most parents operate from the belief that their children know what they are doing. That somehow their children mischievously decide not to do something and then create clever excuses or plausible cover stories to justify their behavior. This seems to be a reasonable way to construe their children's behavior because adults may, from time to time, create plausible cover stories themselves. Adults may procrastinate on an important task and create excuses to tell the boss, but all along being quite aware of exactly what they are doing. It is easy to see why most parents would expect their children to know exactly what they are doing, too, and see procrastination and forgetfulness as phony and somewhat shoddy attempts to manipulate them. Such adult-level manipulation is a misunderstanding of the real situation for children who are Procrastinators.

Procrastinators are only rarely aware of their negative emotions of anger, resentment, and revenge seeking. Most of the time they suppress their awareness of these feelings and any emotions that are associated with anger. Quite often, these associated feelings include discouragement, hurt, insecurity, low self-esteem, and disappointment. Such children become cut off from themselves and communication between themselves and their parents diminishes greatly. These children's lack of self-awareness is motivated by avoidance of painful introspection, and they will fight attempts to help them to become more aware of themselves and more direct in their self-expression. To avoid confrontation with themselves, they will remain compliant and nice on the surface, but will harbor a subterranean defiance and opposition to the requests and demands of others.

The goal of Procrastinators' motivation and behavior is to transfer the unwanted and threatening feelings of anger to someone else. It is not they who are angry, but the others around them. In this way, children focus on the anger of others and not on their own behavior, feelings, and motivations, and perceive themselves to be anger-free, and then feel justified in not doing what people want because people are always picking on them.

In schoolwork, for example, parents of these children usually use power, such as threats and punishments (or even overwhelming incentives), to get their children to do their work. These children outwardly comply, but perform their tasks with such inefficiency or so slowly that parents become angry and scolding. When parents express their anger or become more dictatorial, these children feel unfairly treated, which usually leads to further episodes of underachievement. The whole process may become a vicious circle of underachievement and parental reactions that maintain the very behavior and attitudes the parents would like corrected. By failing to uncover their children's real feelings and motives, parents merely perpetuate the farce of underachievement rather than deal with the real motives and feelings underlying their children's behavior.

Procrastinator patterns of behavior break the bonds of communication and understanding between parents and their children. Procrastinators feel, rightly or wrongly, that their ideas are never heard by significant others. They feel they always have to bow to the authority and rules of others, or to others' ways of doing things despite their own ideas. They experience this bowing to pressure as humiliation and respond to it with resentment. They do not openly express resentment due to their fear of the consequences arising from the perceived power differential between themselves and adult authority. Instead, their usual response is to seem to comply with demands, but do so in ways that ensure ultimate failure. They may perform only part of the task, but not all of it. They may conform in the short run grudgingly, but fail to comply in the long run when the vigilance of authority fails.

When Procrastinators' motivational patterns emerge, a power struggle is created. The power struggle is the relationship these underachievers establish with parents, teachers, and bosses. It is a struggle these youngsters almost always win, simply by failing, whereas helpless parents or teachers must actively strive to motivate or coerce them to achieve.

Further and more insidiously, power struggles and self-defeat become the very relationship underachievers establish with themselves, with their own needs and desires. Even when engaged in something they want to do, these underachievers may sabotage their own efforts by procrastination, dawdling, and forgetfulness at crucial moments, especially when success may hang in the balance, and only their efforts would make the difference.

At other times, Procrastinators may be engaged in some difficult activity that is important to themselves. Usually, in these circumstances, most of these children will feel inner pressures to perform well. When frustrated, they may become angry at themselves and may actually be heard to berate themselves negatively for making mistakes and show other signs of negative behavior and self-hostile emotions. In these cases, performance almost invariably diminishes noticeably as they respond to themselves the same way they respond to adult authorities whom they perceive as critical. In other words, Procrastinators become discouraged children because they use the same patterns against themselves they use against others, even when pursuing self-chosen goals. This is the tragic flaw in these children. They arrange to restrict their own lives but feel victimized by others or circumstances, when all along they are the secret masters of their own fate.

As these underachievers get older, these patterns harden and they cause a difficult and painful conflict not easily resolved. On one hand, these individuals are so discouraged that they feel hopeless and experience much anxiety when they are asked to function autonomously. As a result, they develop a deep but hidden wish to be totally taken over and told what to do in their lives. On the other hand, they have an equally strong fear of just that very thing happening. Their conscience and their ideals demand autonomy and independence of action, while at the same time, they are dependent on the supervision of others to make sure they finish ordinary life tasks. This conflict between independence and dependence becomes the axis around which turns their destiny in everyday life.

As older adolescents, their lives may reflect little or no purposes of their own. They may have few if any goals developed from an understanding of their own values, wants, and desires. Instead, Procrastinator underachievers tend to develop negative autonomy. That is, they define themselves in opposition to others; their sense of self is not defined positively by their own values, wants, dreams, and ambitions for life, but negatively by their passive resistance and opposition to the wants, dreams, and ambitions of parents or others in their lives. It is as though these youngsters were saying to their parents, "I do not know who I am, but I know I am not you."

Classically, these underachievers are quite dependent and set traps for concerned parents. Traps that maintain the very dependency the parents wish to change. Two types of parents or teachers have a great deal of trouble with Procrastinators. These are the authoritarian parent and the unassertive parent.

Procrastinators are especially good at entrapping in endless power struggles the authoritarian parent or teacher. The authoritarian parent or teacher believes in the use of power tactics, whereby youngsters are forced into obedience. Power tactics, such as grounding, study hall, detention, threats, or punishments, usually serve only to evoke passive resistance more forcefully and entrench these youngsters in their "best" coping mechanism. The authoritarian parent usually fails to help solve these problems because procrastinators become more dependent and more defiant all at once. The unconscious message of all power tactics is "I will control you," which is what these underachievers most desire and fear. They resentfully comply with power for now, sabotaging themselves even more later on. Thus, things become worse, not better.

The other type of parent who is least successful with these youngsters is the unassertive parent. The unassertive parent constantly gives in to their child, such as by not following through on discipline demands or by being too inconsistent. Procrastinators are actually made worse by the failure to set limits. The "leave them alone so they can experience the consequences of their actions" approach will not work with these students because they will always believe failure resulted from something they had no power to change. As a result, they do not learn from failure, and basic problems become even more entrenched.

Change Goals

There are two major goals in changing Procrastinators. One is to help these youngsters learn healthier and more appropriate ways of asserting aggressive feelings and anger. Two is a change in the parents' relationship and style of parenting with their youngsters.

The parents will usually need to establish a broader relationship with the youngster that involves sustained encouragement. At the same time, parents must set nonauthoritarian but assertive limits. The parents' demeanor must invite a relationship other than power, and they must spell out the relationship they want.

Patience and persistence are required with these underachievers, especially when they unreasonably criticize people in positions of authority. Parents must constantly interpret the children's underlying feelings of anger, resentment, and dependency conflicts to the child. It is critically important to remember that Procrastinators are not aware of their own motives or conflicts and may be quite unaware of the nature of their problems. It is up to the parents to strike a balance between these children's need for dependency and appropriate limits and to help these kids have insight into their own motivations.

Chapter 5

The Hidden Perfectionist

The characteristics of the Hidden Perfectionist are a pervasive pattern of perfectionism and rigidity of responses in several areas of life. These youngsters are not obviously perfectionistic in their work habits. Their work is often sloppy and ill-prepared. Rather, their perfectionism is hidden in their self-expectations and in their judgment about what others expect of them. They have internalized idealistic expectations about what they should be doing or how they should perform, but they do not believe they can live up to those ideals. They also have high, but often ambiguous, ideals about how they ought to feel, think, and behave, but they often lack much awareness of how they actually do think and feel about things. Being afraid of making mistakes, these youngsters are often preoccupied with trivial details, stubborn, controlling of others, hindered in expressions of feeling, conventional, indecisive, and unable to relax. Two major components of the Hidden Perfectionist are worry and compulsivity. The mixture of these components helps define a particular individual underachiever even further.

The worriers are youngsters who constantly think about things and almost never get them done. They worry incessantly. They are students who, when given an assignment in class, worry about it all day until they finally get home and collapse from exhaustion because they have worried so much. They will be excessively concerned about the details of an assignment while unable to see the big picture. Their worry may become so relentless they become obsessed with ideas or concerns they cannot shake.

These underachievers are often indecisive and unsure of what is the right thing to do. They may be so worried about being correct that, unless there are clear directions to follow, they may become paralyzed by the ambiguous intellectual demands of the teacher (or boss). Ambiguous intellectual demands may include term papers involving topics that demand higher order thinking where conflicting points of views must be integrated and where a range of potential solutions must be identified and selected on the basis of creativity and insight. The perfection-istic underachiever faced with such a task will ask endless ques-tions regarding vague, open-ended assignments, such as how long the paper should be, how many words, what color of ink, and may demand that the teacher tell him or her exactly how to proceed.

The worrying type of underachievers often have good inten-tions, but they may think about their good intentions so much that they may never get around to action. A father once told his son to put his tools away when his son was finished using them. The next day, the father found the tools in the yard next to his son's bicycle. When the father confronted him, his son indignantly responded, "I was going to do it!"

The compulsive component indicates youngsters who are excessively rule-bound and rigid. They feel driven to do things, and rarely, if ever, derive pleasure from school or work activity. In the primary school years, these students may make very good grades due to their fear of breaking rules. Often honor students, they slowly come to experience decreasing pleasure and satisfaction from effort and success. Rather, these students feel "forced" to do work, as though someone else was making them work against their will, even when work is voluntary. Whenever these students feel anxious about something, such as schoolwork, they will often develop repetitive behavior patterns that defeat productivity. Children who sharpen pencils numerous times before starting to work and then have to arrange the papers on their desks just right exhibit examples of self-defeating compulsivity. The preparation for work becomes more exhausting than doing the work itself.

Sometimes, parents or other observers fail to notice how perfectionistic and driven the Hidden Perfectionists actually are. Their perfectionistic qualities are often masked by the symptoms of underachievement. As underachievers, their work may be sloppy and disorganized, but in reality, the sloppiness and lack of organization derive from their resentful resistance to the feeling of being somehow "forced" to do required work and follow others' rules against their will. At times, very good students with consistently high marks in school will also take no pleasure from success, but will continue working anyway because they feel it is expected of them.

Many Hidden Perfectionists will tell a counselor that their

parents expect them to be perfect. Their parents may be praying for Cs, but the youngsters heartily believe that if they do make Cs, then their parents will expect Bs. If they make Bs, parents will expect As, and so on. They believe they can never be good enough for their parents, whereas, in fact, it is the voice of their own conscience that demands perfection, not solely that of their parents. Sloppy work and poor grades are born of their desire to escape the perfectionistic demands of their own conscience. Rather than begin the journey down the road to all As and no mistakes, they will refuse to set foot on that road at all. In essence, they have a sit-down strike in school and then feel discouragement and shame because they are not living up to their own performance ideals.

It is interesting to observe perfectionism in action in the way these students construe simple assignments. Typically, in treatment these youngsters are assigned a time monitoring sheet. At the top of this sheet are the names of all major subjects and down the left side are the dates for two weeks. The children are simply to mark in the column under the subject heading the amount of time, in minutes, they actually study each subject each day at home after school. The purpose of the assignment is to see how much time they really spend on each subject each week. These monitoring sheets will be used for their own decisions regarding how much time they may wish to allocate in the future. In other words, what time they spend in work is totally up to them. Invariably, the Hidden Perfectionist will construe the assignment in perfectionistic terms and come to feel they should write down the time they should have spent on each assignment versus writing down the time actually spent. They will feel guilty and resent the task, often failing to do it for a variety of flimsy excuses.

A Hidden Perfectionist was once told that if he spent thirty minutes on math, he was to write thirty in the column under math on the day he spent the thirty minutes. The next week, he "forgot" to bring in his monitoring sheet, just as he "forgot" school assignments. As his decisions and behavior were explored, he angrily exclaimed how it was unfair to expect him to spend thirty minutes a day studying math when he did not always have thirty minutes of math homework to do. Typically, he had taken a mere example, perceived it as a demand, and then reacted to his perception and not to reality at all. Without understanding this youngster's perfectionism, a concerned adult would be lost in trying to fathom the child's motivations.

Complications

Hidden Perfectionists are quite self-discouraging. They are constantly under the pain of self-doubt and fears of disclosing their weaknesses to others and proving once and for all just how worthless they are. Their sense of low self-esteem and poor self-concept may be masked by arrogance, but their sense of worthlessness is real, driven as it is by perfectionistic self-demands and the feeling that perfection is expected of them by significant others in their lives. Under these conditions, these underachievers believe in their heart of hearts that they can never be good enough, no matter how hard they try, and yet they still feel compelled to try. Under such pressures, children may become quite discouraged and their efforts in the class-room will diminish correspondingly.

Depressed moods often accompany the Hidden Perfection-ists' lifestyles. These students, despite appearances to the con-trary, are often excessively moralistic and can be made to feel guilt and shame quite easily. In adolescence, depression may be masked by complaints of boredom, fatigue, or excessive sleep. Although these adolescents may appear to be "laid back" and relaxed, this is often merely a posture these youngsters assume on the outside. It is usually easy to demonstrate in counseling or psychological testing that such individuals are inwardly re-stricted in emotional expression, tense and anxious, overly sen-sitive to criticism, and distressed.

Test anxiety is often another complication of perfectionistic individuals in school. Due to perfectionism, students feel any-thing that comes from within them is of suspect worth, and on exams, they tend to doubt their own memory. Test-anxious individuals will focus on their anxiety and self-doubts instead of attending to the test itself. When an answer does not come to mind, these students may feel panic and block on other questions, resulting in poor grades on exams. Often, parents and teachers are as frustrated as these students because, in more relaxed times such as studying at home, these youngsters can demonstrate mastery of the subject matter. Self-doubt and per-fectionism often lie at the roots of test anxiety and poor test performance.

Finally, these underachievers can be excessively moralistic and portray their behaviors and that of others in moralistic terms. Actions and demands of parents are seen as fair or unfair, right or wrong. When these youngsters feel treated unfairly, they use their morality as justification for underachievement and opposition to the demands of authority, even if opposition means self-defeat. To the eternal frustration of parents, these youngsters can engage in the most self-defeating behavior and still feel morally justified in doing so because it is right.

One young man was detained in a class for a few moments at the request of his teacher. He made it to his next class on time, but did not have an opportunity to stop at his locker to pick up the work that was due for that class. The teacher would not allow him to go to his locker during class time, and further, took off five points from the grade for the late assignment, although she would accept it late. At this, the young man became highly indignant and refused to turn in the assignment at all, for which he got a zero. He also missed several other assignments out of anger over his teacher's haughtiness. When asked why he failed her course, he replied that she was unfair and did not deserve to be a teacher. As is typical with most perfectionistic underachievers, he seemed to find at least one teacher a year whom he felt was either stupid or unjust enough to warrant his indignant lack of cooperation and poor grades.

Causes

Often, perfectionistic individuals are secretly terrified of being exposed as weak and dependent. They are afraid of being judged as inadequate by their peers or colleagues, of being embarrassed, or of failing to achieve up to the ideals and standards demanded of them by others.

In response to these anxieties of exposure of weakness, real or imagined, the perfectionist denies doubts about himself and develops a compulsion to follow rules and to control himself and others through the often rigid enforcement of those rules. A perfectionistic executive, for example, may demand of himself to always be on time to meetings, and feel pride over how he conforms to time schedules. One executive, however, took pride in always being five minutes late to every meeting. The perfectionist makes rules as to how he will conduct his day, spend his emotions, deal with others in his life, and raise his children. His work has a pleasureless, driven quality to it, and often, so do his relationships.

As parents, perfectionistic individuals are critics. They make up a great many rules for their children to live by, and as these rules often carry an overly moral imperative, these parents are often harsh in their criticisms of their children's misbehavior and failure to conform to parental rules about toilet training, bedtime routines, meal times, and playing with toys and other children. Children are taught that they are naughty when they do not follow the rules and expectations of their parents, even when the children's own wants and needs are ignored in favor of rule enforcement.

Moral imperatives like "should" and "ought" tend to dominate the parents' thinking about their children's behavior. Too often, the children of perfectionistic parents do not feel understood or heard by their parents. Following rules becomes more important than understanding.

Healthy functioning families actually have few rules. The rules they do have are often so shared and so well understood that they are rarely articulated. In fact, healthy functioning families make up the rules as they go along in response to changing emotional personality needs of the children. These families operate through intimacy, shared understanding, and common points of view. Parents are able to listen to their children, who, because they are used to being heard by their parents, talk about their feelings, desires, and needs, so that communication is relatively open and honest. The parents integrate the children's points of view with their own more mature points of view so that what emerges is a consensus of how the family will function. In times of stress and change, self-disclosures and intimacy between family members usually increase, and from this the children and parents arrive at new living patterns.

In a family dominated by perfectionistic patterns, rules become the predominate way in which parents and children relate to one another. Parents make up most of the rules governing their children's behavior. The children are supposed to obey the rules whether they want to or not, and obedience becomes more important than the children's needs, wants, or ideas about how they should act, and usually become more important than shared emotional intimacy, self-disclosure, and understanding. Over time, children come to resent the rules, but they never openly confront and resent their parents directly. They just resent the rules, instead.

As the rules proliferate, and they most assuredly do in perfectionistic families, enforcement becomes increasingly difficult. Communication breaks down and tensions rise in the family. Intimacy and understanding are eroded and the rebellion and anger may escalate into a series of episodic family crises throughout childhood and adolescence, making the family life rather miserable.

Blind obedience to rules without feeling individually understood or at least thoroughly heard is dehumanizing and humiliating to children and to almost any individual. Even if the children obey, they usually withhold belief in the parents' reasoning behind the rules. This may make matters even worse because obedience does not mean children understand or accept their parents' point of view, as parents often mistakenly believe. Further, compulsive parents are generally able to out argue their children, at least until their children's cognitive development shifts to more adult levels at adolescence. Being out argued by superior parents is also humiliating and demeaning to children and are poor ways to achieve consensus within a family.

Children and adolescents in perfectionistic families learn early that following rules is more important than communication or even more important than what they, themselves, believe, think, or feel. As children grow in such an atmosphere, the danger is that they will come to suppress the emotions, thoughts, and beliefs that are discordant with their parents' views and rules in the children's drive to gain their parents' approval and love. These children grow up without much connection to their own inner experiences and have a very difficult time establishing a sense of identity that is separate from their parents and that allows them to face life with courage and confidence.

Resentment and anger over being forced to follow the rules is a common outcome in families where parents govern too rigidly by rules and expectations untempered by empathy and understanding. Children from such families may come to resent any place or institution that is governed more by rules than by personal relationships. Since school beyond the fourth grade is often governed more by rule than by empathy, these children resent school and may become rebellious enough to fail or underachieve despite high intelligence. They don't achieve their potential because of their inability or unwillingness to adapt creatively to rule-bound classrooms and rigid school demands.

The inner experience of Hidden Perfectionist underachievers is influenced by an enduring conflict. On one side they are dominated by the "shoulds" and "oughts" of conscience internalized from their parents. Their conscience makes them feel driven to work to high standards, even to the point of sacrificing pleasures. On the other side, when they do what they should, they are not doing what they really want. Their conflict can be put into these terms: They are constantly concerned over being good and doing what they should do versus being naughty and doing what they want. This conflict becomes cyclical, alternating between "shoulds" versus "wants," and is often reflected in behavior and grades such as seen in the alternation between As and Fs in the same classes. The schematics of the conflict may be illustrated in the following manner.

The Hidden Perfectionist knows what he should do in school, but when he does his schoolwork as he should, he feels as though he is working for others. Even when he works on his own, he usually feels "forced" to do the work. Further, he feels that his work may not really be good enough, anyway. He becomes so grade or results oriented in his work that he derives little satisfaction or pleasure from learning. As a result, the more he works at what he should be doing, the more he feels resentment.

In most underachievement situations in the home, this internal conflict is played out in family patterns between underachievers and their parents. In many cases, the parents' responses to underachievement make matters worse and block these underachievers from becoming aware of their inner conflicts. The parents become the ones who articulate the strictures of conscience by demanding obedience to values and evoking both guilt and resentment in their children. These types of underachievers respond to such parental pressure by rebelling and largely doing only what they wish. The power struggles between parents and children reflect the children's inner conflicts. As long as the inner conflicts remain as external conflict between a child and his parents, these inner conflicts are never resolved and may harden into a lifelong achievement problem.

Hidden Perfectionists are overly involved in approval seeking of parents. Despite appearances to the contrary, these individuals never grow out of their problems without help, even if they are able to overcome underachievement later in life. In truth, career achievements may actually mask continuing underachievement problems. For example, the successful executive or professional who is dependent on his secretary at work for organizing him and dependent on his wife for everything at home reveals an individual whose success is not a result of autonomy and maturity, but results from dependency on others to support and control his life.

Even if Hidden Perfectionists do well, the pleasureless, driven quality of success eventually robs life of its meaning for them and creates strains in their relationships with others. Often, appearing as a male achievement pattern, these men become fathers whose emotional restrictions and stinginess creates problems between themselves and their male children, leading to a common pattern of successful fathers who have unsuccessful, underachieving sons. The sons act out their fathers' own, secret dependency needs through underachievement in school.

Change Goals

The major change goal for Hidden Perfectionist underachievers is to lead them to their inner conflicts and to help them regulate those conflicts appropriately. One of the key aims is to first connect these students with their feelings: the anger, anxiety, and shame or guilt typically suppressed by these underachievers.

As they learn to experience what they feel versus what they think they should feel, these underachievers begin to understand the conflicts between their thoughts, values, feelings, and behavior. Increased self-assertion and emotional self-disclosure strengthen these youngsters' ability to manage their own affairs, set goals, and decisively move forward in realistic, creative ways. Once these goals are accomplished, most of these youngsters reveal themselves to be capable of very deep and rich feelings and able to make clear, abiding commitments to other people and ideas in life. When they mature, these youngsters will usually show keen interest in careful analytic thinking and intellectual achievement.

Being a parent to these underachievers is often complicated by the need of these individuals to control their relationships with others and not let others have an influence over them. In this regard, these types of underachievers share motivational characteristics with the Procrastinator underachievers. Hidden Perfectionist students may also be shy and hypersensitive to rejection and criticism and are prone to misinterpret the constructive remarks of parents that are intended to help them. Much of their underachievement and frustrating behavior may be traced to their desire to revenge themselves for perceived unfair or critical treatment at the hands of parents, teachers, or others. Revenge seeking in these underachievers is often difficult to stop due to their strong sense of righteous indignation and moral justification of self-defeating, revenge-seeking behavior.

Chapter 6

The Martyr

The essential characteristics of Martyr underachievers are a pervasive pattern of repetitive, self-defeating behavior that, at times, may become extreme. They often fail to accomplish tasks that would further their progress toward important, especially self-chosen, goals. They defeat themselves despite their ability to accomplish those tasks easily. These underachievers snatch defeat from the jaws of victory. Students who help other students do well on a science project but do not complete their own projects are one example. These underachievers tend to choose friends and date individuals who treat them poorly and are bored with those who treat them well. These are the individuals who reject reasonable offers of assistance or help from others. This rejection may range from polite refusals to an almost cunning sabotage of efforts by others to be helpful. These youngsters are especially frustrating to teachers who take these students on as a project to help them reach their potential in class. The more the teacher treats these children well and offers help, the more likely the students are to fail and get worse. Under pressure, these youngsters may improve for a while, but they will inevitably fail to turn in crucial work and so sabotage their own and their teachers' efforts.

These youngsters also react to success with increased discomfort. They fear and avoid sustained success. Grades may rise to excellent levels only to fall suddenly and apparently without warning just when things seemed to be turning around. Praise and reassurance are seen as embarrassing and tend to evoke negative emotions, such as sadness or anxiety. In certain cases, praise and reassurance are disbelieved and are totally ineffective, while in other cases, praise and reassurance may render these youngsters so uncomfortable that their behavior actually gets worse.

These youngsters tend to have short-lived enthusiasm. They begin pursuit of a goal with good motivation, but as soon as their efforts seem to be leading them to success in their chosen endeavor, they lose interest in the activity. Martyrs often do well in school at the beginning of the year, only to wind up seriously underachieving later. They may begin music lessons, only to lose interest and quit just when effort seems to be paying off. They lack insight and they are discouraging to themselves and others in the extreme.

Such a self-defeating behavior pattern often places a great deal of stress and tension on important relationships. Characteristically, Martyrs seem to be children adults can help. Initially, Martyrs receive the help offered by adults enthusiastically, and some positive changes invite further commitments from helping adults. Soon enough, however, Martyrs begin to fail again in a way that evokes anger and a desire to punish or dominate the children. Often, the helpful adults find themselves ill at ease with their feelings of anger and desires to punish Martyrs, leading them to reject these kids instead. Teachers, for example, who take these types of underachievers on as a project may wind up literally hating these youngsters and at the same time feeling guilty for wanting to reject them, too. The desires of teachers and others to punish Martyrs is often the reciprocal of the youngsters' relationship with their parents, and is due to the way Martyrs seek to punish themselves and others via failures and underachievement.

I once conducted a workshop on underachievement with a group of high school teachers and counselors before the start of school in August. In the preceding year, the administration of the school decided to take the six best teachers in the high school and assign them to teach forty students who were identified as severe underachievers. These students were bright and capable of doing well, but chronically failed or nearly failed their classes. The six teachers committed themselves to help these students by giving them the best of their teaching commitment and creativity. As these teachers described their efforts and the characteristics of the students, I became convinced they had been trying to teach forty Martyr underachievers. The more these teachers tried to salvage these students, the more defeated and angry the teachers became. By the end of the school year, results were poor. Only a few of the students were actually helped, but all the teachers were burned out. In fact, these teachers refused to ever teach such classes again and even threatened to leave the district if they were ordered back into the classroom with those students.

The Martyr is the most severely disturbed motivational and personality pattern associated with underachievement problems in school and career. The more this pattern predominates in an individual, the more difficult and problematic his life becomes. This pattern is most associated with the failure of all kinds of help, whether help is medical, psychological, or behavioral. Failure is due to the strong proclivity of Martyrs to punish and defeat themselves and others through failure to reach attainable goals. The diabetic who continues to eat sugar improperly and the victim of lung cancer who continues to smoke cigarettes are two examples of this pattern.

Martyrs also tend to emphasize their own particular weakness and shortcomings to others. In school, they may emphasize and act out academic and personality shortcomings that make it difficult for them to succeed. They may complain that they really are not as smart as others believe them to be, despite evidence to the contrary. They claim powerlessness concerning their behavior, as though they cannot help what they do. These youngsters maintain the view that they are helpless and cannot prevent themselves from daydreaming during exams or sleeping in class and are powerless to prevent procrastination.

The self-defeating behavior patterns are characteristic of the long-term functioning of Martyrs. Depressed individuals characteristically show these self-defeating patterns of behavior and attitudes, and Martyrs are often depressed. However, when the depression lifts, the self-defeating personality style of Martyrs remains, whereas in others, the self-defeating lifestyle may go away entirely. Furthermore, the lack of success of the Martyrs lies in their inability to handle the insecurities of success itself.

Causes

Certain parenting patterns are common in the families of Martyr underachievers. In the early years, from birth until about seven or eight years of age, at least one of the parents is dominating and punitive whenever these children make mistakes or do something the dominating parents do not like. These children learn to bond to the dominant parent via punishment and pain and feel insecure when they are on their own. When these children are doing well on their own, they tend to be ignored. To seek attention, they then mess up, and in swoops the dominating parents to pay attention to them, only the attention is usually negative and punitive, such as shaming and scolding, and sometimes even physical.

Quite often, parents do not understand what they are doing. They just see their children as difficult, willful children, and live by the philosophy, "spare the rod, spoil the child." By physical punishment, shaming, and harsh scolding, they are inadvertently reinforcing the very behavior they wish to change.

These parents often tell me about the early and current training of their children. One father told me that his son is disrespectful and mean until he gets a whipping. After that, he is the sweetest little kid, very helpful around the house and respectful. However, it never lasts, the father complains. He always gets mean and disrespectful until the father has to whip him again. This is the Martyr-creating cycle.

In school, Martyr underachievers may do well for a while on their own, perhaps, but then begin to feel nervous and worried. No one pays much attention to them when they do well. So they will fail to turn in assignments or do other things in the class to gain parental attention. As soon as the parents find out about the bad grades or misbehavior, in they come with punishment once more. Martyr underachievers seek failure so they can reestablish security contact in the best way they know how, no matter how damaging it is to their development. These kids do not know what they are doing to themselves. Literally, they sacrifice their success in life to meet their dependency needs and to feel secure.

Later in life, what was once a punishment-security link between parents and their children becomes part of the identity makeup of the children. That is, the Martyr pattern becomes internalized and functionally autonomous from the punitive actions of the parents. What this means is that when these children are successful, they feel more insecure and frightened. When they fail, they feel more secure. Thus, failure leads them to feel secure as failure symbolically reconnects them with the dominant, powerful parent.

As a consequence of the internalization of parents' child rearing style, Martyr underachievers have established a negative link between pleasure and success so that success does not evoke satisfaction, evoking instead anxiety, guilt, and even depression. Awards, promotions, and good grades can so increase anxiety and discomfort that these individuals may panic if success comes unexpectedly and suddenly. The student who unexpectedly makes an A+ on one test and fails the next two is one example of a Martyr pattern. The executive who suddenly wins a promotion and becomes depressed and almost gets fired is another example of the negative link between pleasure and success. Success brings pain. Failure brings security. For Martyr underachievers, the old adage that success is itself a motivator for more success could not be further from the truth. Martyrs snatch defeat from the jaws of victory every time.

A typical example of the Martyr pattern occurs when a youngster complains of boredom to his parents, but can think of nothing he would like to do on his own to make those feelings go away. The parents may make numerous suggestions about what their youngster can do to get rid of the boredom, at which time the Martyr complains that none of those suggestions appeal to him. The parents may then dominate the youngster by making him do something anyway. The problem of dependency is perpetuated while seemingly trying to solve it. In this way, the youngster remains dependent on his dominant parents through failure to solve his own problems independent of the parents.

Change issues

Breaking the ties that bind the Martyr underachievers to the powerful, dominant others in their lives is the key to change although this is a difficult objective to achieve. Martyrs define themselves by their submissive relationship to the dominant parent. They see their failures and lack of success as crucial to their own security needs by maintaining the dominance of the significant parent. Independent functioning may evoke so much anxiety and insecurity in the Martyr and in their parents that both gladly sacrifice true autonomy and independent functioning to escape the pain of anxiety. This sacrifice by the dominating parent is experienced and construed by both parents as being a result of concern and love for their children who, in turn, are seen as too incapable of facing the dangers of the world alone. As a result of these patterns, Martyrs reach the teenage years too enmeshed in the domination-submission cycle of the parent-child relationship to have formed their own independent identities, values, and goals in life. They cannot pursue life with the hope of increased autonomy and sustained success.

Most Martyr underachievers do desire to break the patterns of dependency, and their lives often reflect a kind of compromise within themselves. They do not break away from the dominance-submission cycle due to the intolerable anxiety associated with true autonomy, so they develop negative autonomy. Negative autonomy gives Martyrs a feeling of freedom while at the same time actually binding them to the dominant parent. Negative autonomy is usually expressed in Martyrs when they act in ways that make other people who are concerned with their welfare feel helpless and incompetent. Martyrs will express independence by not letting others help them, but never actually refusing their help or rejecting it openly. Martyrs appear to accept aid from others, only to sabotage such aid in ways so frustrating and maddening that the persons trying to provide the help actually become rejecting and give up. In this way, Martyrs maintain some independence by covertly refusing help and yet maintain dependence through underachievement, thereby avoiding the terror of breaking with the dominator in his life.

Martyrs' inner emotional life is often a cauldron of rage over their submission to being dominated and punished. This rage rarely sees the light of day because to express rage openly may lead to rebellion and an end to dominance. Their rage is given some outlet in provoking others to feel rage toward them. The

Martyrs' own anger is kept under wraps and is never allowed to propel them into a separate and independent emotional life.

Martyrs are prone to negative reactions: what should help does not. Usually, negative reactions are mild, but they may become severe enough to be life threatening. Some of these children become depressed or suicidal as they begin to change their patterns. Thus, negative reactions must be constantly analyzed. It also is important to eventual success that teachers and parents recognize the limitations of trying to help these kids. Parents and teachers should not be drawn into feeling guilty or angry at these children's seeming lack of success or progress. Rather, teachers and parents must maintain a steady availability to Martyr underachievers. To be truly helpful, they must have endurance and a strong sense of self-worth that is independent of the Martyrs' successes or failures in life.

Chapter 7

The Shy Type

It is difficult to overestimate just how much these extremely sensitive, Shy underachievers fear embarrassment and humiliation, and how concerned they are about how others judge them. These underachievers are easily hurt by criticism and sometimes by even the slightest hint of disapproval. Seeking the approval and acceptance of others and avoiding social humiliation is the primary motivation of these students. Their poor school performance and social shyness is related to their deep-seated lack of self-confidence, fear of disapproval, and fears of negative evaluations from others. These youngsters tend to avoid new situations for fear of possible disapproval and will engage in challenging tasks only when assured of success and approval. Thus, they are prone to poor academic and career achievement even though they possess excellent abilities. They are especially prone to failure when academic challenges involve the possibility of increased social contacts, or when success could lead to increased demands or responsibilities they fear they may not be able to meet. These youngsters usually make their highest grades in classes that require limited social contact or in which they feel their teachers genuinely like them no matter what the grades. Often, these youngsters fade into the woodwork in school, rarely asserting themselves in class, and may find the normal changes from one level of school to the next higher one quite difficult. For Shy students the move from elementary school to middle school may be especially difficult and under-achievement issues may first emerge clearly into the open during this transition time.

As a rule, these youngsters have only a few close friends or confidants outside the family. They are reticent in social situations for fear of saying something embarrassing or inappropriate and are petrified of appearing foolish. Many times Shy underachievers feel humiliated when parents call teachers at school to check up on their progress. They rarely mention such feelings to their parents for fear of even further disapproval. The fear of negative evaluation may be so strong that these youngsters can become quite impaired in many areas of social and academic functioning.

Underachievement results from the fears of negative evalua-tion and avoidance of rejection and humiliation. Shy under-achievers fear failure and attendant embarrassment so much that they protect themselves from real failure, which would be a personal humiliation and disaster for their self-esteem, by avoiding school tasks, homework, studying, and other success-oriented behaviors. Ironically, these students bring about the very failures or poor achievements they most fear. By not really trying, however, Shy underachievers have a face-saving excuse: they fail from lack of trying, not from lack of intelli-gence or some other potentially humiliating self-deficiency.

The fear of failure and humiliation runs so strong in the motives of these students that they may simply shut down in the face of challenges they feel they may not be able to meet. This is especially true for those youngsters whose parents place a strong value on intelligence, good grades, and educational achievement.

Shy underachievers tend to develop phobiclike symptoms in response to academic and life challenges. In fact, some of the characteristics of a clinical phobia can be seen in the attitudes and behavior of Shy underachievers. Those who suffer phobic reactions to snakes, for example, experience extreme anxiety and even panic when in close physical proximity to a snake. To a lesser degree, shy students experience similar anxieties when in a situation where they expect disapproval or humiliation. The phobic individuals who fear snakes would avoid snakes on many levels: avoiding thinking about snakes, avoiding reading about them, avoiding pictures, and even avoiding the areas in which snakes are likely to be found. Likewise, Shy underachievers will tend to avoid achievement demands on similar levels: they may experience difficulties in studying for exams they believe they may not do well on; they may "forget" important deadlines; they may experience test anxiety and block on exams due to phobiclike avoidance of the tests. They avoid thinking about schoolwork, assignments, or even studying for tests. Some youngsters find it very difficult to keep their minds on tests and homework assignments. They slip into daydreaming and are unable to force themselves to work or even focus clearly on exam questions. Such students may daydream a lot, especially when they are not doing well or expect to fail. Actual school phobias may develop in such youngsters wherein they suffer anxiety attacks associated with physical proximity to school and may refuse to attend school at all.

Shy underachievers usually make themselves dependent on others to help them do schoolwork. They avoid facing new or feared challenges alone by arranging circumstances so that their parents become overly involved in their everyday school tasks. These youngsters may not begin studying without constant reminders. Once they start studying, they tend to daydream or pop up and down out of their chairs so much that their parents often feel it necessary to make them sit still and focus their attention on the work. One shy youngster complained that he made good grades only when his mother helped him study, and when he made poor grades, it was because his mother failed to help him study enough. In this case, the mother's overinvolvement in school and his dependency on her helped to soften the humiliation of potential failure because his mother shared responsibility for failure. Unfortunately, he could not take full responsibility for his successes because she shared those, too.

It is not unusual to find that Shy underachievers develop phobic symptoms to a variety of situations besides school. They may have nightmares, become overly shy about dating, going to parties, or other social activities. They may have difficulties going to job interviews or with self-assertion in general. They may be prone to developing agoraphobia, so that venturing from the home to a shopping mall may become an ordeal necessitating the summoning of a great deal of courage; even then, they may not be able to do so without being accompanied by a trusted member of their family or a close friend. The more shyness patterns pervade students' lives, the more dependent on parents these youngsters become, and naturally, the less open they are likely to be about their thoughts and feelings. Shy underachievers may be isolated, lonely and easily discouraged in their lives.

Causes

Shyness patterns of avoidance of challenge and fears of failure, humiliation, and embarrassment usually arise early in childhood when parents become overly critical and push their children into mature and independent functioning beyond these youngsters' capacities. In such situations, too much shame and humiliation is evoked in children who are not yet capable of avoiding shame by conforming to parental demands. This may happen, for example, when parents push children into early toilet training or independent bedtime before the children are emotionally ready. They are not allowed normal dependencies. These children internalize negative criticism and feel so ashamed of their failures that they fear new situations due to expectation of further shame and humiliation.

In reverse, overprotective mothers who do not allow normal distresses and anxieties of growing up to occur may communicate to their children that they are helpless and dependent and need Mother to protect them. Invariably, overprotective parenting creates anxieties in children about being separated from parents, so that as a rule, children of overprotective parents are excessively dependent on parental involvement and attention. Eventually, in the case of Shy underachievers, parents become critical and shaming of the very dependency the parents have helped to create, while the youngsters try to hide their true feelings out of fear of further shame and humiliation. In these cases, both parents and children pay a heavy price for anxiety and dependency as anger and shame come to dominate family life.

Change issues

One of the initial complicating factors in helping this type of underachiever lies in getting them to commit to being helped. They resist talking about their school problems because they fear that such discussion will be yet another situation where they face the possibility of negative evaluation. Parents must make the decision to make effective changes to help, but herein lies the other difficulty. Many times, one or both parents of this type are secretly partners in the youngsters' avoidance of challenge. These parents overprotect their youngsters from experiencing anxiety or emotional frustrations and tend to wrap them in a protective cocoon. These parents may literally fret for years before finally doing something effective to help their children with underachievement problems, only to procrastinate on making effective changes. Such parents may have strong fears of embarrassment and need for approval as well and become overly concerned that their children will somehow reject or become angry with them. If counseling is needed, parents fear being seen as failures because by seeking professional help, they irrationally believe they are giving up on their child. In some cases, parents fear the possibility of a negative evaluation by the counselor concerning them and their parenting, and may not want to face feeling uncomfortable themselves.

Parents or teachers who wish to help these children must be on guard to avoid committing two potential mistakes. First, they may be tempted to push these youngsters too fast, beyond what they can do or feel they can do, thereby evoking a pattern of fear and shame that may have originally caused the emergence of the shyness patterns in the beginning. Second, parents or teachers may inappropriately protect these underachievers and never expect them to experience anxiety beyond that which was originally comfortable. This would create the same protective cocoon originally created by the overprotective parents and defeat change.

These types of youngsters are prone to develop mild depressions later in the teenage years. These depressive episodes are usually linked to marked social anxiety and continuing school problems. These youngsters learn to overcome depression as they learn to overcome fears of humiliation and develop more assertive patterns of success striving and social contacts.

It is often the case that successful change in Shy underachievers will necessitate successful change in the parents on whom these children are psychologically dependent. The parents must let go of their children. Expansion of peer group relationships and the formation of friendships outside the family are often crucial to successful work with these children. Change in shyness and avoidance patterns must occur by a kind of pacing process, whereby a youngster is encouraged to maintain a level of anxiety he can handle without creating a situation where anxiety becomes too great, as in the confrontation of fearful challenges and new situations. Shy underachievers must maintain some contact with what they fear and learn to identify the factors that inhibit their lives and achievement motivations. In this general manner, Shy underachievers can be guided to establish for themselves richer social lives and greater academic successes.

Chapter 8

The Socialite

This type of underachiever is a great socializer and cares very little for careful, analytical thought and intellectual achievement. They are often able to tolerate school because of the opportunity for visiting friends school hours provide. They go to school to be popular, gossip, show off clothes, gain attention, and act as class clowns. They do not go to school to learn and meet academic challenges. Socialite underachievers love novelty, seek excitement and stimulation, and fatigue easily when having to conform to routines that call for delayed gratification of their social wants and desires. These individuals are often lively and are prone to exaggerate and overly dramatize whatever they are feeling at the moment, the intention of which is usually to draw attention to themselves or manipulate others to get their way. They enjoy being the life of the party.

However, their affability and charm are often illusory, a facade that hides anxiety and self-doubt. Socialite underachievers' need for approval, praise, and attention from others is often achieved at the cost of their own long-term self-interests, educational goals, and harmony in the family. Their need for attention and approval may be so strong that they become angry and depressed if these needs are not met. Their social charm may give way to flashes of haughty anger or dramatic moodiness and irritability. If they believe they cannot gain positive attention to help them ward off negative feelings and self-doubts, they may resort to gaining negative attention. In fact, these students may orchestrate emotionally intense, dramatic scenes with parents, wherein these youngsters may beg, plead, employ emotional or moral blackmail, anger, and in severe cases, even suicide threats to gain their way, especially if parents have grounded them from being with their friends.

It is a mistake with these youngsters to assume that their emotionality and easy sociability reveals depth in their relationships. In reality, they tend to be self-centered and egocentric in long-term relationships such as with boyfriends or girlfriends and parents. They are often overly concerned with physical attractiveness and become fashion plates in school. They may dress to gain attention for themselves. Further, they tend to be social chameleons: their attitudes and behavior may change depending on the type of peers whose approval or attention they seek for the moment.

Their boredom with routines; their need for attention, reassurance, praise, and approval; their poor tolerance of frustration; and their need for quick gratification of their impulses often lead these youngsters to focus on short-term gains and benefits at the expense of long-term goals. In education, these students spend too much time socializing or talking on the phone and not enough studying. They may regret poor grades and the resulting tensions in the home, but regret does not alter their future behavior. Despite good intelligence, they often resent reading and will actively fight against it when made to do so by concerned parents. These are the students who resist tutoring and feel that study skills are a waste of their time . . . unless they turn tutoring and study-skill training into social events. Underachievement may result from their boredom with routines and low tolerance for frustration. Intelligent youngsters in the teenage years may sacrifice good grades for popularity and social acceptance, never really believing that intellectually competitive individuals can be socially popular as well.

Socialite underachievers are surprisingly very competitive. In some respects, their popularity is based on being socially competitive with other peers. While they may appear to have many friends, often their friendships are more characteristic of shifting alliances and may show a marked lack of emotional intimacy. In fact, early peer groupings of these youngsters reflect a large component of hostility rather than warmth and affection. Motivations for developing friendships are not based on mutual respect and self-disclosure among compatriots, but upon developing a rather temporary alliance within one group of peers or an alliance against the perceived restrictiveness of parents. In this way, the peer group may encourage and support behavior that leads these students into conflict with parents or other out-group peers.

The competitiveness and self-indulgence that color the socialites' peer relationships often lead them to feel lonely and alienated. These types of youngsters have difficulties being alone to engage in solitary pursuits, such as academic learning. These are the types of students who feel they just have to be around others, and when alone in their rooms, are most likely to require a radio to remain alone or studying for any reasonable length of time. They will easily sacrifice study and homework for telephone conversations with friends, not only when in secondary school, but even in college where many of their peers begin serious career strivings.

Causes

These types of underachievers have learned to hide their true feelings from others and to put up a false front in order to gain the approval and attention of parents. In the adolescent years, they may transfer those strong approval-seeking motives to peers and teachers. When socialites feel the need to gain attention, it is usually in the service of warding off depressive feelings and loneliness. In the classroom, these individuals often become the class clowns, and when they succeed in getting the class to laugh at them, they momentarily feel less lonely. However, the class clown antics do not satisfy the craving for approval and the need for deeper relationships, and often class clowns are punished for such behavior by poor grades and increasing tensions in school and home. Thus, class clowning actually increases the socialites' sense of loneliness and depression.

In the first six or seven years of growth, bright and sensitive youngsters may develop an oversensitivity to the attention and praise of parents. These youngsters turn much of their attention to following the rules of their parents and become quite upset if they get disapproval. During the course of time, these youngsters learn to hide feelings they believe their parents do not want them to have. They try to display only those attributes their parents like or appear to want. They learn the parents want bright, cheerful, pleasing, and charming youngsters. Parents reward with attention and approval the physical attractiveness and sociability of their children and try to maintain their children's good moods by giving in to demands and manipulation and providing material goods. Such children respond to this parenting style by hyper-vigilance to subtle signals of approval-disapproval from parents. They can become so focused on their parents that they literally do not realize what they are feeling or thinking. They see material goods, getting their way, having things done for them, and attention as signs that they are worthwhile and loved. They see punishment, disapproval, or discipline as signs of rejection or disapproval or as devaluation of worth. Over time, they increase their attention to external signs of approval and social appearances. Their emotionality becomes shallow or lacking in detail. This lack of depth and detail can be seen in their emotional expressions and styles of speech, which tend to be impressionistic and dramatic, but sometimes little else. For example, socialites may describe their friends as "just fantastic," but be unable to go beyond that expression to describe richer experiences.

One of the core personality problems Socialite underachievers have is a deep-seated belief that they are inadequate to handle life on their own terms. From this belief, they draw the conclusion they need others to handle life for them. Recognizing their low self-esteem is too threatening and painful, they try to get other people to esteem, notice, and admire them. In this way they can feel better about themselves and avoid taking on their inadequacies honestly and competently.

Both the Shy underachiever and the Procrastinator under-achiever have core self-perceptions of being inadequate to handle life, too. However, both of these other types of underachievers draw the conclusion that it is best to back down from challenge. The Shy underachiever actively avoids anything that may expose his feelings of inadequacy, and the Procrastinator sets other people up to push him into being adequate. By contrast, Socialites actively set about making sure their needs are sufficiently met by others. They actively seek attention and approval of others and may do almost anything to be noticed. They use their wiles to get other people to do things for them and are very manipulative of others' feelings to secure the attention and approval they need. The Scarlet O'Hara character in *Gone With the Wind* is an example of a female of this type, and Willy Loman in *Death of a Salesman* is her male counterpart.

Socialites may become so radical in their need for external approval from others that they become looking-glass people. That is, they always see themselves as they are reflected in the eyes of others. They may feel they are as other people think them to be. If other people show them attention and compliment them on their looks, they believe they are charming and beautiful. If others criticize or reject them, then they feel worthless and inferior. In fact, it is common for Socialite under-achievers to value external events over their own internal experiences so much that they are left, over time, without a clear sense of identity apart from how other people react to them. They see themselves primarily in relation to other people. The long-term obsession over how others think and feel leaves them empty and easily bored and prevents them from learning to deal with their own inner thoughts, values, and emotions. They have no rock within themselves on which to stand, so they turn to others to be the rock for them.

Socialites have very little insight and, in fact, are often frightened of questions that lead them to introspect. Anxiety over recognition of their inner sense of inadequacy leads these types of underachievers to develop a vague cognitive style. They cannot remember specifics about their own past behavior. They love vague, impressionistic memories and phrases because by keeping things vague, they do not have to acknowledge inadequacy within and change. However, without specific knowledge about their mistakes, they will never have enough information about themselves to take charge of their behavior and become more competent.

Complications

Parents, teachers, friends, even their counselors, may fail to realize that these underachievers are really becoming depressed. Socialites have good social skills and are usually quite good at appearing to be cooperative, friendly, happy children despite deepening self-doubts and depressive moods. The smiling charm becomes the mask that hides true desperation. They may smile through a depression and increasingly lack the ability to concentrate and suffer shorter and shorter attention spans. They are cooperative and helpful at home, but may keep a diary that reveals how angry and enraged they are at other people toward whom they appear outwardly friendly and may even admire. Boys or girls may come to focus on physical attractiveness and on physical relationships rather than emotional relationships and may even engage in premature sexuality in a misleading attempt to gain intimacy and approval. Poor grades and failures usually result from sacrificing grades for social popularity, which eventually bring punishment and disapproval from parents who value education and good grades. In an attempt to help with this problem, parents may resort to grounding from social activities. However, grounding only deprives them of one outlet for getting rid of depressive moods. As a result, these youngsters may become more uncommunicative with parents and deepen their resentment and possible rebellion when away from home. Thus, parental devices to solve school and discipline problems only make matters worse.

Change issues

These types of underachievers need someone who can help them come to identify and explore their hidden feelings. Essentially, this entails reflecting back to these youngsters the emotions underlying their behavior, even if the emotions and motives are not obvious. For example, it is often helpful for the class clown if the teacher interrupts this behavior by saying, "I can tell you are feeling pretty bad today and need my attention." It is surprising how this response sometimes brings tears to the eyes of some students who may secretly feel gratitude that someone has noticed just how lonely they really feel. These types of responses unhook underachievers from their symptoms and invite them to connect with the details of their own emotional experiences.

If these youngsters can be brought to better self-understanding and a better sense of competency, they may become real assets to their community and family. If responsible, they can develop rich and deeply meaningful social relationships and may be quite creative and imaginative. When they do not alter approval and attention-seeking behavior to form a deeper identity and learn to sustain achievement, they usually remain seriously underachieving in their careers as well as egocentric, demanding, and shallow in their relationships with others.

Chapter 9

The Con Artist

The Con Artist type may be the most difficult of all under-achievers for parents and teachers to understand. These are the youngsters who seem to have a great deal of charm for their age, especially around adults. They know how to make people like them and how to appear warm, poised, and confident. They seem to have so much going for them, except the ability to work. Parents and teachers mistakenly focus on the charm and social ease of these youngsters as valuable, positive gifts and not as symptoms of what is wrong with these individuals.

Con Artists want something for nothing. They want good grades, but do not want to work for them. They would prefer to charm others to get what they want. They are always making deals with people in authority to extend deadlines, grant them special favors, or to manipulate them to get what they want from authority. However, these underachievers never intend to follow through on their end of the bargains. They believe they are very special people who can and should be granted special favors, and they should not have to honor their side of an agreement in order to get what they want. Typically, however these kids will feel greatly abused if the other party to an agreement, such as Dad, fails to follow through on his part. Con Artists believe they can get what they want simply because they want it, not because they have earned it.

Their social charm hides a self-centered tendency that may be extreme. They live basically for their own gratification and feel especially entitled to have things their way regardless of the rights, needs, and obligations of others. As long as they get their way, they are charming. When they are refused what they want, they can become angry and aggressive and may attempt to intimidate others into giving in to them. Intimidation may include giving parents or others "the silent treatment" or even getting worse in behavior and attitude until the exasperated parents are worn down and tired enough to give in to their demands. Con Artists are also good at waiting parents out. They feel that if they can simply wait long enough, then Mom and Dad will loosen up on discipline and things will go back to normal again; meaning they will once again get their way.

These youngsters are often consummate manipulators of other people's feelings. They are good at evoking guilt in others over supposed unfair treatment and then argue or bargain their way to get what they want. In fact, these youngsters' basic attitudes toward parents and adult authority is that adults are fools. When caught in a failure to follow through on commitments, these students may turn to legalistic hairsplitting in an attempt to convince their foolish teachers and parents that their motives are sincere. These are the types of youngsters who make parents and teachers feel like they need to write everything down in black and white so that there can be no further "misunderstandings" regarding what is required of the youngsters. Unfortunately, contracts never work with these children because they disdain authority and are self-indulgent and faithless regarding commitments. Basically, other people do not have the same rights and are seen as a means to the fulfillment of their own desires.

These youngsters can be made to feel remorse and regret over their actions. However, their feelings of guilt and remorse do not help these youngsters change their behavior in the future. They repeat the same old patterns over and over again. Yet, remorse and guilt are the only hope for these children.

Con Artists have developed a mask of charm and sociability, even of interpersonal sensitivity, which they use to gain selfish desires. Desires tend to be rather simpleminded: they want a phone in their room, curfews extended, a chance to go to a forbidden party, or more money or other freedoms, but without increased responsibilities. However, as time goes on, Con Artists often discover needs and desires that demand more complex behavior, greater personal intimacy, and greater responsibility. It is in the more complex demands for intimacy and honesty in long-term relationships where Con Artists experience anxiety, failure, and personal inadequacies that are not relieved through manipulation. The mask of superiority and social charm fails, and what is left exposed are individuals who feel inferior, depressed, and empty.

Con Artists are essentially lonely, emotionally isolated individuals. They can manipulate feelings in others, but may not really empathize with the feelings of others. They understand loyalty and are often quite jealous in their relationships, but they have more difficulty experiencing love and compassion in others. These children tend to interpret love and compassion as masks that hide ulterior motives. Some of these children have more severe problems experiencing and understanding the depth and range of interpersonal care and warmth common in intimate human relationships. These kids are outsiders looking in on the warm, human, emotional drama, but are not able to participate fully in that drama themselves, even if they wish they could. Like Scrooge in Charles Dickens's classic novel *A Christmas Carol,* they peer in from the cold to the warmth of Bob Cratchet's family, unable to enter or participate with them.

In school, when Con Artists miss deadlines, they are likely to bargain and make deals for deadline extensions, but if not watched carefully, they will likely miss new deadlines as well— all with very good, even plausible excuses for why deadlines are missed. If a teacher or a parent confronts this behavior and their excuses, the Con Artist may become very manipulative and even emotionally blackmailing so that it is not they who feel the guilt of their misbehavior but the teachers or parents. Con Artists are very good in working other people for their own ends, even if that means getting parents or teachers to argue among themselves about the proper way to discipline, while these underachievers get off scot-free. They are masters at getting other people to do their work whenever they can, thus avoiding the real challenges of work or school.

Causes

The psychological features of Con Artist underachievers are the development of grandiose fantasies about their own self-worth that far exceed any actual accomplishment. Their grandiose sense of self-importance leads them to expect special entitlements, favors and notice from others. They tend to exaggerate their talents and accomplishments and brag, sometimes to the point of alienating others. They tend to be preoccupied with fantasies of unlimited success, power, and brilliance, and to be consumed by envy of those who are more successful or powerful than they. Reality plays little inhibiting role in these youngsters' fantasies. They are going to the best colleges and they will make lots of money; yet, they have failed algebra twice and are in the bottom quarter of their class. Since they are so talented, failure cannot be their fault; hence, they blame others for their failures.

Parents tend to feed the development of the problem in two ways. First, the parents are overprotective and set few limits for their children. They become Little Caesars of the nursery who can do no wrong and are allowed to run roughshod over other kids. They are very often given their way and may only rarely be made to suffer the consequences of their actions or obey their parents, and even then, parental discipline is often inconsistent. The parents essentially adapt to the youngsters' demands, not the youngsters to the values and limits of the parents. From this parenting style, youngsters may grow to perceive care and love as weaknesses to be exploited, not as values to be copied, learned, and lived. As they grow into adolescence, these youngsters may substitute power motives for love, manipulation for trust, and may fail to learn the subtleties and rewards inherent in reciprocal and intimate emotional relationships.

Secondly, these youngsters often get out of work and chores through manipulation of others. For example, they are the youngsters who will break a few dishes when it is their turn to wash so that, eventually, the exasperated parents either perform the task themselves or assign it to the more responsible siblings, who they know will get the job done right.

All underachievers create lack of success for themselves in school and, later, in their careers. However, Con Artists bring to their lack of success in school a certain sarcasm and disdain for work that is especially irritating to parents and teachers. Their attitude is that they could do the work but they do not want to because it is too boring or beneath their real abilities. Often these kids claim they are ready for college and will make plans to attend the best universities. These youngsters, as a way of compensating, will claim they are brighter than most of their peers or teachers, or will find some other trait they are better at and focus on that trait as a source of pride and contempt.

Con Artists believe they are special and should be entitled to privileged treatment. They feel they do not have to wait in lines; they want rides when convenient for them; and they refuse to work for certain employers because the work is "beneath" them. They require constant attention and admiration and will often seek social offices in clubs or positions that offer them the admiration of others.

Fantasies of success are substituted for real success as they shun the effort required to bring their fantasies to reality. When goals are actually pursued, they show no pleasure in their work or success, unless they are able to accomplish tasks easily, without effort. Ambition and even achievement cannot satisfy their grandiose sense of self and fantasies of achievement.

The self-esteem of these youngsters may be surprisingly fragile. One day they seem on top of the world, the next day they are agitated, irritable, and sometimes depressed. They fish for compliments from others and may develop a very charming social presence that easily wins initial friendships. However, as these social acquaintances begin to deepen in demand for emotional intimacy and personal self-disclosure, the Con Artists' fragility begins to show. Under the demands of long-term intimacy, the facade they use to fake their way into admiration and friendship cannot be maintained. Others begin to see through their act. Empathy may be almost totally lacking in more severe cases so that others find them uncaring and even cruel, especially during those times when others may need reciprocal emotional commitment.

Interpersonal exploitation in which Con Artists take advantage of others for their own goals or ends, usually self-aggrandizement, is common. In romantic relationships, these individuals choose partners with little or no true caring but who bolster their own self-esteem or gratification. Often, romantic relationships are viewed like a chess game, in which there is no real sincere desire for love and exchange of warmth, but as moves that are made to trap the other person and control the relationship. A male may show special interest in a girl only until she begins to reciprocate, and then he ignores her so that she is manipulated to become more committed to him than he is to her. As one seventeen-year-old male Con Artist once explained: "I really turn on the charm and treat a girl as special. When I sense the girl falling for me, I like to act real cool to her. That way, if she keeps trying hard enough, someday she'll be good enough for me. That is the way I get my way."

Change issues

Con Artists generally resist effective help. In order to change, these underachievers must confront the distance between fantasies and realities. Con Artist underachievers tend to mask fears and weaknesses by feigned indifference that exasperate and frustrate attempts to help, and may, in more severe cases, be almost impervious to attempts to help them. As a result, helpful change can take a long time, and only the most enduring and committed of parents or teachers will be successful. In severe cases, the parents give up first. They can see no real changes in the youngster after extended efforts or even formal psychological treatment.

The establishment of a consistent external discipline is crucial to successful change. Systematic consequences must be worked out between the parents and, if possible, with the school, so that these youngsters pay a consistent price for substituting fantasies for real life successes. In mild cases, the youngsters, under a tight structure, become irritable and test limits in subtle ways, such as arguing that a particular teacher is boring, or they do not need the credits in that teacher's course anyway. More severe cases may refuse to cooperate, and may even get worse to punish their parents or intimidate them into returning to old patterns of parenting more comfortable to the Con Artists' taste. When these tactics no longer work, then some level of depression and anxiety clearly emerge, and these children can face their fragile self-esteem. As in other cases involving the successful change of chronic underachievement problems, the parents must work hard and change first.

Chapter 10

Things That Fail to Help Underachievers

When parents come to my clinic, they believe they have reached their last resort. After a year or more of trying this or that technique, this or that form of advice of friends or schools or well-meaning family members, a plethora of educational techniques, motivational tapes, subliminal suggestions, power tactics, deals of various kinds, tutoring, and other forms of temporary bandages to staunch the wounds that stubbornly refuse to heal, and just before giving up, they come in looking for a new set of answers. The amazing thing to me is how parents cling to old ways that fail even as they seek to learn new answers to old problems. I have learned in ten years of treating underachievers and their families that before a new approach can work, those who work with a child must first understand thoroughly what will *not* help underachievers overcome their problems.

Years ago in my undergraduate career, I came across a tale that wonderfully illustrated the appropriate attitude for encountering something new that one wished to understand. I do not even remember today where I read about this, but from memory, the tale went something like this.

A professor of anthropology from a Western university wished to understand Buddhism and traveled to the East to talk to a Zen master. As the anthropologist sat before the Zen master, he was thinking of all the things he wanted to know about, when the master offered the professor some tea. The professor graciously accepted the offer of tea, but the Zen master set a full cup before the professor and, without further ado, began to pour more tea into an already full cup. Of course, the tea immediately spilled from the cup into the professor's lap. The professor grew perturbed and demanded to know the reason for such treatment. Reportedly, the Zen master replied with what I imagine was a kindly smile, "You have come to find answers to your questions, but in order to understand the answers I would give, you must first empty your cup of the old so that you can fill your cup with the new."

Logic

Logic will not work with an underachiever. Carefully explaining how important grades are to a child's future is useless. Underachievers are discouraged children who habitually sever the connections between today and tomorrow; between today's procrastination and tomorrow's failure. Children who will not work for a teacher they do not like will not understand why they should turn in homework no matter what the teacher is like. Logic and wisdom do not motivate children to work consistently, no matter how well delivered, no matter how inspirational. Parental lectures about the value of hard work, motivation, and success are ultimately fruitless.

Now, I am not saying that lectures and logic do absolutely no good. There is little harm in repeating good advice and good values as often as a parent deems them suitable. By the time children are in their teens, however, they have memorized most of the lectures parents can give, no matter how much creativity and emotionality parents muster in their delivery. Most kids have heard it all before and know what the parents will say next. You can tell this when teenagers' eyes begin to glaze over a few minutes after a lecture begins.

A mother once told me that her husband spent almost an hour in an extended lecture with her son. When the husband came to bed, he excitedly told his wife how he believed he'd finally gotten through to his son and reported his talk blow by blow. The wife knew better, however. For a few days, her son did evidence better motivation in school and certainly seemed inspired to work harder. After a week, however, the inspiration became like a New Year's resolution, more honored in the breech than in the fulfillment. Underachievement behavior and attitudes reemerged as strongly as ever before.

In my office I once listened to a father give his daughter an inspired lecture on responsibility. I noticed that she began to fiddle with her fingers. I stopped the father and asked his daughter if she knew what her father was driving at. She finished his lecture for him.

Most children and teenagers already know the way things should be done, the way they should think and act in school, and why academic success is important. My rule of thumb is that if the parents value education and success, then the children will have absorbed those values as well. The problem is that underachievers do not follow through on what they know.

The carrot and the stick

The carrot and stick approach to student motivation are really forms of power designed by parents to get what they want from their children: achievement behavior and better grades. External rewards for good behavior and externally imposed punishments for inappropriate behavior will not help most underachievers learn to motivate themselves to work for success. Sometimes rewards and punishments even backfire and make matters worse, such as when children perceive rewards and punishments as bribery or coercion. Kids can fight the effects of rewards or punishments by engaging parents in seemingly endless power struggles that lead to nowhere but frustration and tension.

Let me describe a typical situation where the parents decide to offer something to their child that they believe he wants: money. They decide to pay money for grades. Any amount will do, but let us say they decide to pay $10 for every A, $5 for every B, $2 for every C, nothing for a D, and fine him $10 for every F on the report card. Now, to be fair, they offer the same deal to the higher achieving siblings. At the end of the grading period, the high achieving siblings have broken the bank and the underachiever winds up owing the parents money.

It does not matter what the bribe is, underachievers wind up failing to get the bribe or they turn the bribe into a struggle of some kind. I knew a father once who offered his son a fancy sports car if he made straight As on his report card. This young man was quite intelligent, but he was taking courses that he could easily do well in. He was repeating his toughest class, algebra, and making an A in it when the deal was struck with his dad.

The son really buckled down for three weeks, but failed to turn in some assignments and made three As and three Bs, his best report card in two years. Was the bribe working? The father thought so.

The son wanted a new deal from his father, however. He argued correctly that he had just gotten the best report card in years, proof he had turned things around. His new deal was that if he could repeat the three As and three Bs, he should get the new car. His father, pleased at having finally found something his son would work for, agreed.

However, by the end of the second grading period, the As were now Bs and the other grades were Cs. The son argued that the grades were still really good and said that if he could be given another chance for the car, then he would make it. Only, now he wanted all As, Bs, or Cs, or as he put it, a B average. The father agreed.

By the end of the last six weeks, the son brought home a report card with a D in algebra, an F in English, one B and the rest Cs. When asked by his father what had happened, the young man replied that he did not really need that car since his friends could drive him anywhere he wanted anyway.

Sometimes parents use the stick approach by punishing or grounding to motivate their children to get better grades. Taking away privileges or grounding kids from activities is a time-

honored but largely ineffective way of influencing student behavior. Grounding and punishments inevitably fail to help kids
learn how to motivate themselves to achieve.

I met a young man who was finishing the eighth grade after
a year of barely making passing marks. I met this young man
in mid-May, after he had been grounded every weekend since
mid-October after his first poor report card. This young man's
problem was that he failed to turn in homework, and his major
excuse was uncontrollable memory losses. He "forgot" his assignments, his books, the notes from teachers, and almost anything else related to school. He did, however, manage to make
good grades on tests. He was a good kid, not a rebel or a
troublemaker.

His parents devised what they thought was a rational carrot
and stick plan. All he had to do to avoid grounding on an
upcoming weekend was to turn in all his homework the week
before. They did not put any emphasis on the grades he made
on his homework, or even whether it was entirely completed.
All he had to have were no zeros on his homework, and he
earned his freedom. Unfortunately, every week from the start
of October to the middle of May the next year, this young man
had managed to forget at least one assignment, thus grounding
himself for the year. Interestingly, when I questioned him about
his perception of his parent's approach, he complained bitterly
about them. He felt they were unfair to keep him from his
friends all year. He told me he could not help it if he had a
memory problem.

I could go on with examples of the failure of rewards and
punishments to alter underachievement and poor motivation

in children and teenagers. The point is, these approaches have no lasting effect on the children whose futures are at stake. In fact, I have become convinced over the years that grounding alone has an especially bad effect on the emotional maturity of discouraged children. As I have stated earlier, dependent functioning is characteristic of underachievers. When parents ground children or teenagers, what is the message the children receive? Stay home. And when the children are grounded, who else is grounded along with them? The parents! The message of grounding is for children to remain dependent. The message the parents send by bribery is exactly the same: it is the parents who control rewards of success, not their children who control the rewards. The parents teach "other" control, not "self" control. If the parents remain in control, then they foster the very dependency they are hoping to eradicate, and thereby inadvertently help maintain their children's underachievement.

The other major problem with rewards and punishments, besides not working, is that children are encouraged to work for the wrong reasons. They work for money, for a car, or to avoid punishment. They are not working for the satisfaction that comes from honest work, from learning difficult subjects, or from achievement. The objects used for bribery, whether parental praise or money or cars, are the incentives. Is all we want for our children that they work only for the things they can get for themselves, the incentives? Do we not really want them to work for the intrinsic pride and self-esteem that comes from setting their own goals, summoning courage to make commitments to challenges, overcoming obstacles, and gaining achievement for themselves? What will it profit our children to gain all our rewards, our cars, our praise, our granted freedoms, and avoidance of our punishments, only to never discover or develop themselves?

As parents we must be careful to watch what we teach our children through the methods we use to rear them. In the families of many underachievers, rewards and punishments come to dominate the relationship between parents and children during the school year. The parents forget that their first and primary job in helping their children with chronic motivational problems is to understand what drives their children to underachieve to begin with, and then work to change those self-defeating motivations. Rewards and punishment often take the place of understanding, with the result that the child becomes deeply discouraged and resentful. He may come to perceive his parents as not caring about him but only about his grades. Such children often feel dehumanized and will seek revenge by stubbornly refusing to give the parents what they seemingly want most, even if it means sabotaging their own futures.

I recently worked with one such child. He was a sixteen-year-old in private school on a partial scholarship due to his outstanding athletic ability. However, he was flunking out of his second private school and was about to lose the advantages his athletic abilities had provided for him. He was an angry young man, especially toward his father, who used rewards, punishments, logic, and lectures as the primary way to relate to his son. Now, in my work with this young man, he was able to admit to me that revenge was what motivated him with regard to his father. He arrived at that insight with me after months of treatment effort.

Unknown to me, the father had offered his son a car for good grades. A car made sense in this family for both parents worked and a car for their son would have been convenient. The mother wanted him to have the car regardless of grades, but the father was adamant. However, the son figured he could wait out his father and get a car anyway. He never shared his motives with his parents and continued to just get by in school. Finally, his parents sent him to summer school in a desperate effort to get him to raise his grades. He did well enough in school to earn the car, but before his parents bought him the car they had picked out for him, he was caught cheating in school. He had earned his grades the easy way, it seemed. In a clever twist, he told his parents that they did not trust him. He said he would work harder if they showed they had faith in him. In this way, he induced his mother to get him the car despite his grades, and the father went along with the mother.

When I found out what had happened, I questioned the son about his thoughts. He said with evident pride: "I won. I knew if I waited long enough I would get the car anyway." I raised the issue of growing up, which had been a topic of treatment on many occasions. He replied, "Look, I'm sixteen years old. I've got the rest of my life to be responsible. I want to be a kid as long as possible." What the parents had rewarded was cheating, irresponsibility, and self-defeat. What they thought they were rewarding were grades. How sad for them all.

Tutoring and other educational approaches

Specialized educational-skill training that includes tutoring and study skills is a typical way that parents attempt to mend the problem of poor grades. The assumption behind tutoring and study skills training is that kids who make poor grades simply lack the appropriate skills necessary to make good grades. Once those skills are learned, then grades will rise. Tutoring is a good approach for motivated students who are trying, but are having trouble learning material in a class. Special training in reading and studying are worthy of all young students to ensure educational skills are part of students' adaptive abilities. Yet, for students with underachievement symptoms, no amount of study skills training or tutoring will overcome poor motivation and lack of effort.

Tutoring fails to help underachievers for a variety of reasons. One important reason is that most underachievers may have already learned the material the tutor is teaching. In my experience, many poor students actually score grade level or above on standardized achievement tests but still make poor grades in school. They have learned but do not give their knowledge back to the teacher when it counts, such as on homework or tests.

Another reason for the failure of tutoring to help, even in the cases where a real skill deficit exists, is that tutoring is usually conducted in small groups or in a one-on-one situation. Underachievers do better when supervised one-on-one because of their dependent functioning. With a tutor, underachievers do well for a while, but when the tutor goes away, the effort and grades eventually fall once more. Tutoring does not and is not designed to solve the problem of dependent functioning that plague underachievers and their families. In fact, because most tutoring is a highly supervised, one-on-one experience, and because some underachievers actually do better for a while with a tutor, tutoring may thus inadvertently increase the very dependency from which underachievers suffer in the first place. Far from helping youngsters overcome dependency, tutoring may actually reinforce that dependency and make matters worse. This may be one explanation for why the parents of underachievers seek out tutoring year after year. Tutoring may get a child through a class as a temporary bandage, thus meeting the parents' desires for their child to pass, but it does not resolve the causes of underachievement. When underachievement returns, the parents go back to tutoring and the endless cycle begins all over again. Nothing really changes. Parents use tutors because it is all they know to do.

Let them suffer the consequences

I call this approach the "Little Bo Peep Theory" of underachievement. The rationale of this approach goes something like this. Nothing else has worked. Tutoring, logic, lectures, groundings, rewards, bribes, praise, homework sign-off sheets, pleading, power tactics, and supervised involvement of parents and other responsible adults—all of these have failed to help. The answer must lie in the parents backing off and leaving their children alone. This way, the children can suffer the consequences of their actions and learn a lesson. Maybe then they will eventually grow out of their problems. Leave them alone and they will come home, waving their As before them!

The answer to this theory is simple. If you let a thief continue to steal, does he learn to become an honest citizen or just a better thief? The Little Bo Peep approach to underachievement rests on the mistaken belief that underachievers will learn from the consequences of their actions. This is decidedly not the case. Underachievers do not learn from success how to sustain success the next time, nor do they learn from failure why they failed and change what they do the next time challenges reappear. They keep repeating the same mistakes over and over again. To back off and do nothing just lets them continue to go down the tubes.

Underachievers do not learn from their experiences because they substitute excuses for effective action. Excuses keep underachievers from knowing the decisions and motivations that led them to fail. Without knowledge, they cannot change, so when faced with more failure, they simply respond with all they know to do, which is make better excuses. I have worked with children who have failed a grade twice and who then blamed their parents for holding them back, or who have become so discouraged that they gave up.

Further, underachievers do not learn from the consequences of their actions because they do not assume responsibility for themselves. Human beings do not simply grow to maturity like saplings grow automatically to oaks when soil, air, and water are right. The slow, gradual growth of a personality from childhood to adulthood requires the assumption of responsibility. Without the feeling of being responsible, then children will not change the kinds of decisions they make about achievement, they will not initiate changes in behavior or attitudes, and will not, consequently, mature properly.

Chapter 11

Fundamental Principles for Parents

Over the years of helping underachievers learn to motivate themselves, I have found certain basic principles for parents that help them change motivation and underachievement in their children themselves. These basic principles are attitudes parents take toward their children, toward each other, perhaps even toward life itself. These principles parents either come to express during attempts to change their children's under-achievement or they adopt, on faith, in order to make change possible. I have found that when parents lack commitment to these principles, positive changes in children's motivation and achievement are less likely.

Principle 1: parents work together

Parents must be emotionally mature enough to work out their differences with their spouses or other parent and work together for their children's welfare and future success. One of the common experiences in my clinic is that parents of

underachievers usually disagree about how to rear their underachieving child. Sometimes the disagreement lies not only in
how they should act as parents, but sometimes in the very ways
they perceive and emotionally respond to their child. In many
cases, the parents have so polarized their attitudes and approaches one from the other that they may even inadvertently
sabotage their attempts to help their child. The parents of the
Con Artist, for example, often find themselves arguing over
discipline matters while their sons or daughters go on about
their merry ways doing just about what they want. As a result
of parental conflicts, one parent may capitulate and allow the
other parent to control discipline, or they may continue to
fight each other and become too inconsistent to be effective in
changing their children's underachievement patterns.

Working together to solve underachievement problems is so
important that I have developed some guidelines for parents in
communicating with each other. Without guidelines, parenting
underachievers can be even more difficult.

The first of these guidelines is: keep no secrets. Keeping
secrets places barriers between parents, emotional as well as
informational. The keeper of the secrets places himself in the
superior position, and the ignorant parent in the inferior position, the one who is not in the know. Too often, the left out
parent begins to feel like a satellite orbiting in and out of view,
but having no real connection with his children. The one keeping the secrets too often begins to feel guilty about his knowledge and may even come to resent any attempt by the
unknowing parent to become more of a part of the parenting
of his children. This situation can easily get out of hand as the
ignorant parent, feeling left out and useless, usually tries to

assert his authority without enough information and may over-assert himself in ways that are harmful and alienating. Parents, indeed the whole family, may become increasingly emotionally polarized, even to the point of becoming dysfunctional.

In addition, the parent who keeps the secrets gives implied permission to the child to continue problematic behavior. Most adolescents whose parents keep secrets about the adolescents' misbehavior seem to think something like this: "If Mom knows about my misbehavior, and she keeps the secret from my father, I get in no trouble because of it. If I get in no trouble, then, secretly, it must be all right to continue my misbehavior. If it was really important for me to stop doing what my mother secretly knows about, then it would be serious enough to tell Dad and they would try harder to stop me." Keeping secrets between parents almost never works and may indicate serious problems brewing in the family or marriage that need work.

To counteract any tendency to keep secrets, I counsel parents to have talks several times a week where they do nothing but share information about their children. The information should include the nice, cute, funny, and laudable things their children do, as well as the problems and difficulties their children exhibit. If Dad works a lot, or vice versa, and cannot be in tune with the flow of life in the home, then Mom must make the effort to inform Dad about the daily lives of the children, the good and the bad. Without the open sharing of information, parents often go astray. Parenting is hard enough. One advantage of the two parent home, after all, is the wonderful opportunity to bounce ideas and strategies off another involved and caring person. Two informed heads are better than one.

The second of these guidelines is: parents make decisions

together about their children. Parents need to have a lot of communication about the rearing of their children, especially when a child is having chronic difficulties with underachievement in school. The parents have to be consistent in their discipline with an underachiever, and discipline should teach a child basic achievement values. Parents must agree on such things as privileges, extracurricular activities, how they govern a child's time, and the very attitudes they take when things inevitably go wrong. They need to agree on how they will help each other. They must agree on punishment and rewards and exactly what they want their child to develop as part of his character and then set goals and work toward them together. Adolescents usually present parents with multiple challenges, and if parents are not consulting with each other regarding their decisions, then one parent is inevitably left out and resentful and the other carries the unfair burden of being a single parent in a two parent home.

The third of these "working together" guidelines is: parents present a united front to their children. Both parents are seen as being together in their decisions and discipline. Ordinarily, they should never dress down or criticize the other when disciplining or talking to their children. What I have in mind here is one parent, say the father, is dealing with his son about one of his son's problems, and the mother does not think the father is going about the discipline in the right way. She then jumps in and attacks the father for what he is doing or saying, and then the parents start arguing while the son goes outside and plays with his friends. In the meantime, the son's difficulties are forgotten and, quite often, the underachiever learns how to manipulate parental disagreements and fights so that he gets his way inappropriately.

I know that sometimes parents get angry and say things to their children they shouldn't that the parents later regret. I suggest that parents work out a signal, like a "time out" sign, they can give to each other surreptitiously, so that negative moments can be controlled. Further, if parents disagree with a punishment or with how something was handled, they should talk seriously about it later in private. When they have reached a decision together that changes discipline one has imposed, they both meet with the child to present a united front. In essence, parents should see themselves as the king and queen, the benevolent despots of the family, trying to raise their children, the prince and the princess, in such a way that they will take over the kingdom someday. When the king and the queen constantly fight openly over the discipline of their children, it demoralizes and distorts the family and usually leads to anger, fears, disrespect, and other problems in the children.

Principle 2: parents set the values

It is a truism in the psychology of child development that children learn their core life values from their parents, or, more correctly, from their attachment to their parents. If there is a good, loving attachment between children and their parents, the children absorb their parents' values like a sponge. However, they do absorb their parents' values in their own ways, based partially on birth order, genetic traits inherited from parents such as temperament and sensitivity to others, and the developing personality and perceptions of the child.

Children express the incorporation of parental values when they regulate their own behavior in following the "shoulds" and "should nots" of the home. Articulating and behaving in accordance with the internalized values and experiencing the feelings of pride and self-esteem engendered by following those values (or the guilt and shame when those values are not followed), is characteristic of growth of a child's working conscience. A good, working conscience is critical to healthy social and psychological development in general and to motivational development in specific.

Although the incorporation of a working conscience and values is a complicated psychological and social process in infants and children, my rule of thumb is that if early parenting has been good enough in terms of care, consistency, and attachment, then most children by the age of seven years have incorporated their parents' values. If the parents value education and achievement, then the children will have those values as potentials within them, as well as many other values.

Once a child has incorporated his parents' conscience, the real question then becomes, which values will become actualized in the living reality the child creates in his daily routines. Which values will the child care enough to fight for and which values will the parents care enough to work for in their lives and those of their children? These are very crucial questions every parent needs to ask of themselves because, as discussed in earlier chapters, underachievers fail to actualize many of their own critical life values and virtues.

In the home, the parents must set the values by their behavior and the discipline of their children. In many cases, the values the parents set in the home will be those I call the "gut reaction" values. Those values the parents perpetuate by their emotional and behavioral reactions to the vicissitudes of life around them. Often, parents are unaware of how consistently they respond to their children in certain ways that reflect the parents' character, emotional habits, moods, and personal emotional needs, fears, and anxieties. Sometimes, these "gut reactions" inadvertently encourage, maintain, or even cause underachievement. Getting angry at repetitive, irresponsible failures and excuses may reflect a father's frustrations over the failure of his son to live out the father's competitive, achievement values, but this type of "gut reaction" may make matters even worse rather than help children change.

The better situation is when parents try to make their "gut reactions" much more of a controlled, conscious decision about what values they will bring to their parenting. For example, the father may become angry over his son's repeated excuses and failures, but the most profound source of anger may be over the broken trust bond between father and son, and the father's fears that his son may never grow up. If the father focuses his attention on his values of personal accountability and personal integrity and the need for his son to express responsibility values, then he will more likely create a plan of discipline and teaching to reach his son than he will if he just remains angry and punitive. At least the father may seek help and advice if he cannot help his son change.

The essential question for parents, then, becomes what will be the core values the parents will vivify and which ones will they work to instill in their children. When parents talk and work together, as suggested in Principle One, then this question becomes easier to answer. To make conscious decisions to train children in living out values is a much better parenting style than to only use "gut reactions" when raising children. Conscious decisions can grow and change with the real needs of children; "gut reactions" are too often bound up with the unconscious needs and conflicts of the parent and may not grow and change to fit the needs of the children.

Principle 3: make no excuses

Over the years I have discovered that parents make excuses for their children's problems and the children are clever enough to pick these up and incorporate them into how they justify their inadequacies. Excuses make children deaf, dumb, and blind to the fact that they make choices to create problems for themselves and others, and the more they become committed to their excuses, the more deaf, dumb, and blind they are to themselves.

In my clinic, I often see parents before I or my staff sees the underachiever. Parents will tell me things like, "He's lazy," "He's learning disabled," or "He can do his work when he's interested, if not, then he won't do well." These may not look like excuses, but they are. Kids justify their behavior by them. Inevitably, when I next meet the children of parents who have told me such things, kids parrot their parents' explanations as though the children had no control over their problems.

It is best not to give excuses to a child. Innocent sounding descriptions, such as, "He's lazy," do more harm than good. When a father says, "He's just being a normal adolescent" when describing chronic underachievement, his son is likely to appeal to social statistics to justify and excuse his own lack of effort and responsibility. "Most of the class failed that test, too," is a phrase I have heard often when underachievers wish to justify doing very little most of the time.

Worse than giving kids excuses on a silver platter are the excuses parents give themselves to justify doing nothing. As I was writing this chapter, I interviewed two parents about their son. The mother, who was involved in the daily grind with her fifteen-year-old and his school work, was worried about him. She described typical underachievement problems. The father, however, was a successful, busy, and respected lawyer. He said his son was a good kid with good values and suggested his grades were normal since his poor grades and lack of effort seemed to be what a lot of kids his age were doing. This father also said that he was reared to solve his own problems, and besides, his son was just like him when he was his son's age. The implication was that Dad had turned out just fine, thank you; therefore, so will his son.

Despite the father's resistance, both parents agreed I should see their son a few times. In the first session, this young man was typical: a good kid, articulate and bright. However, after I reassured him of the strict confidentiality of our conversation, he told me he had cheated extensively in school for the last two years. Even though his grades were not good, they were as good as they were largely because he cheated on tests and homework and projects. He was finally caught and pledged he would never cheat again, but he was concerned he might anyway. When we explored some of the reasons for cheating, he at first said he did not know. But as we talked a few more moments and I switched the talk to his relationship with his father, he told me he did not think he'd ever be good enough in school for him. Unfortunately, the young man left for the summer and the parents never brought him back in. I wonder if his father ever discovered his son's problem?

Of course, the father had no idea his son had cheated so much, nor how the son felt about never being good enough for him. The father's excuse: "He's just like me," prevented the father from even being curious enough about the differences between himself and his son to be a real father to his son and help him. Unless, of course, the father did know about the extent of his son's cheating and that is what the father wanted to avoid having to face openly.

To be really helpful, parents must give up excuses that keep them from gaining real knowledge and involvement with their children. If parents cannot give up excuses for their children then how in the world can they help their children learn to give up excuses, assume responsibility, and become better human beings? Overcoming underachievement not only helps a child feel better about himself, gain confidence in his future, and have a more open future, but it helps him become a better person. There are no excuses for not becoming a better person.

Principle 4: change the child, not the environment

Underachievement is almost always grossly underestimated, and many parents think that if they just change schools, move to a new neighborhood, or send their child to a military school, boarding school, or to a special tutoring school, then their problems will be solved. In cases where an underachiever is also getting into trouble, a divorced parent may decide the troubled child will do better with his natural father or natural mother, maybe even an aunt or uncle or grandparent.

A change of schools may be helpful under some circumstances, obviously. These would include situations where a school is so dysfunctional as to be physically dangerous to children or adolescents. If a child legitimately fears for his own safety and makes poor grades because of it, then a change of schools is needed to first protect him and secondarily to help him change his ways. Also, if an underachiever is beginning to create other problems, such as an adolescent underachiever who associates with drug and alcohol abusing peers or is beginning to engage in serious delinquent activities, then a change of schools may help break him from his peer groups. Common sense and mature judgment must be exercised in these situations.

However, children and adolescents carry their problems within them no matter where they go, and if these problems are not resolved, then they will likely simply create the same negative environment around them in the new school or new location. The old proverb about changing the clothes does not change the man applies well here.

That change in scenery will make profound changes in the developing character of a child's motivation is the usual hope that is cheated by such moves. The sad fact is that a chronic underachiever has developed a self-defeating motivational style that does not easily change with passing scenes or seasons. All change, for it to last, must come from within the child. These must be changes in the self-concept or the character of the child, changes in conscience and motivation. These changes can only come about when a child has insight into how he makes decisions that lead to failure and to self-defeat and pain. Once an underachiever knows he makes specific decisions to fail, then and only then can he even begin to take control of his own life and work to change himself.

Adults will often talk about child and adolescent underachievers as though these children know they are making decisions that lead to failure. For example, adults may say something like this: "Well, he decided not to do his homework and he decided not to study, so he'll just have to suffer the consequences. Until he decides to do better, nothing we do will help him." As rational as this statement sounds at first, it really begs the question about awareness of decision making.

The real problem is that child and adolescent underachievers are not aware they are making decisions that lead to failure. Only in retrospect or in hindsight do they sometimes acknowledge in a vague way that they make decisions. However, at the time adolescents make decisions not to do work or not to study, they have a head full of excuses and other thoughts that sever the connections between decisions and action, that sever the connection between today and the consequences tomorrow. In other words, underachievers in the moment they make decisions that lead to failure are not aware they are making those failure-oriented decisions. The real help concerned parents can provide for underachieving children is to bring them into acute awareness that the child is making decisions to fail at the moment he is making those decisions.

Without the awareness that one is making a decision, then one is not really free to alter one's destiny and change failure to success. Over and over again in my professional practice, when I focus on an underachiever's actual experiences of failure, never do they really feel a sense of freedom in their failures nor, ironically, in their successes. They perceive failure and successes as coming from forces and circumstances beyond their control. They fail because of such things as "boredom" or because of the teacher or the parents who "constantly bug" them. They succeed because they were lucky or because they had a teacher who made the class interesting for them or because they liked the class for other reasons. Rarely do they see themselves as individuals who make decisions that lead to outcomes. To so perceive themselves as making decisions would indicate a state of true inner freedom and sense of personal responsibility that is often terrifying to these kids, which of course, they then avoid like the plague.

Helping people who have ongoing problems to become aware of how they contribute to their problems is often a difficult task. However, parents who read this book, especially the chapters on change, need to remember that the aim of most of their work is to lead their children into awareness of the decisions they are making. This is the inner change necessary to bring about true freedom of action and a sense of responsibility necessary for any individual to take control of their lives and alter destiny. Otherwise, we will likely be hearing a generation of individuals that T. S. Eliot wrote about in his poem "The Hollow Men."

> We are the hollow men
> We are the stuffed men
> Leaning together
> Headpiece filled with straw. Alas!

. . . Shape without form, shade without colour,
Paralysed force, gesture without motion;

Changing the school or the home without also changing the consciousness of the child, will not likely be very helpful in the long run.

Principle 5: life is tough

Parents must know that life is tough and there are no guarantees for any of us. As parents, we just have to do our jobs with all our might. After all, God gave us these children to take care of and if one of them is a problem, then that is good. God gave us an underachiever to rear so that our lives would be filled with a significant and interesting problem to solve. We have no excuses, either. Our children are our responsibility, and it is up to us to train them and rear them to become responsible for themselves and to reach their potential as human beings.

To change and become more successful, many underachievers will have to suffer emotional pain and low self-esteem. Parents have to know that life is tough, and they may have to allow their underachieving children to suffer without being rescued. Suffering is often unavoidable because underachievers do have a conscience and low self-esteem, though they cover up with excuses and denials. Effective parent discipline will break through the excuses and denials to make children conscious of their decisions and personal responsibility in failure. This is often a difficult, emotionally painful part of self-knowledge that children must go through if they are to get to the other side where pride, self-esteem, and confidence await them.

Most parents know their children must learn responsibility if their children are to become fully functioning adults themselves someday. Yet, over and over again, I find that parents are worried and afraid to allow their children to suffer emotionally so that they can learn the gift and burden of having to account for themselves. Parents too often rescue their children, who, in turn, learn irresponsibility and avoidance of self-discipline and the other primary skills that build character and allow them to reach their potential.

As a psychologist, I find myself having to reassure parents that suffering may be appropriate, indeed, unavoidable, if their children are to grow and improve. One mother's questions were so typical that I have chosen to include them in this book.

Her son had failed the eighth grade, but she and her husband talked the school into passing him to the ninth grade if they sent him to summer school for his most deficient classes. I agreed with the parents that it would probably do more harm than good to retain this bright but discouraged young man. I felt their summer school idea was a good one. Her son was a bright, sensitive young man, a "Hidden Perfectionist" type of underachiever.

As part of our plan to help their son, the mother, father, and I felt psychological testing would be useful. That testing was performed and I gave the results to the parents. I explained how the testing revealed that their son had a perfectionist conscience, felt a great deal of shame and guilt over his failures, but how he had essentially cut himself off from his conscience and emotions by using excuses and avoiding responsibilities. Our aim in treatment was to reconnect him with his own conscience so he could better regulate his behavior in work toward realistic goals and eventually learn to enjoy his work. Part of my work as a professional and theirs as his parents would be to arrange circumstances in such a way as to allow us to confront his excuses and lead him to feel accountable and responsible for his failures (and his successes). I explained that we wanted him to see how his decisions lead him to fail in getting what he said he wanted for himself.

I gave an example. Suppose their son set a goal to bring his science notebook home to study for his science test, on which he wanted to make a B. However, suppose he said he had "forgotten" his science book. Instead of punishment, lecturing, or hopping in the car to go get it, the first intervention would be to ask good "how did it happen" questions. The purpose of these questions would be to find out what he did instead of getting his book, what his thoughts and feelings were about it, and how he was going to solve the problem of his missing book. Another purpose was to find the point at which he made a decision that led to not getting his science book when he could have so that he did not have the excuse of "forgetting" to save face or avoid responsibility. By doing things like this over and over again in many different ways, we would begin to unravel the underachievement symptoms and excuses and reveal to him how he makes decisions that lead him to either fail or succeed.

At the end of my explanation, the mother asked me an important question. "But won't our focus on these things make him feel worse about himself? Won't that lower his self-esteem? He has such low self-esteem already."

In the beginning, I was frustrated with such questions because I felt they betrayed such a fundamental lack of psychological insight. I now see such questions as only those a good parent would ask. Suffering is essential for such a young man, I carefully explain these days. I told this concerned mother that her son was already suffering, but his ways of dealing with it were discouraging him, leading him into a deeper hole, and preventing him from growing more mature as he got older. He was not learning from his suffering how to prevent further suffering in the future. Our job is to have enough compassion to lead him to know that he causes his own pain and lead him to know he can make new decisions for himself. Thus he can become empowered to control his own destiny by making different decisions. As professionals and parents, we help the underachiever make new decisions. There is enough to defeat us in life without adding to the losses life brings by chronically defeating ourselves with bad decision making.

The psychological pain associated with underachievement—the shame, guilt, low sense of worth, feelings of incompetence, discouragement—should not be caused by the parents' actions, but by the child's own behavior. What parents and professionals do to help the child is focus on the correct problems. By focusing on the correct problems, the child is led to discover his own mistakes and develop a sense of personal responsibility for them. When parents attempt to create pain and pleasure by handing out punishments and rewards, such as groundings for bad grades and material rewards for good ones, then most children and adolescents will assign the cause of their pain and pleasure as residing outside themselves in either the withholding or giving parent. Rewards and punishments are most likely to maintain, if not contribute to, the very underachievement patterns parents are trying to change.

Underachievers will rarely focus on themselves as the cause of their own problems, but will perceive the cause of their pain and pleasure as residing outside of themselves in the will and behavior of others. As a rule, they externalize the locus of control over their negative feelings about learning to parents and teachers. "If my parents would not bug me, I'd do my homework on my own!" seems to be their battle cry. But when parents do leave them alone, they still do not do their work. "My teacher does not like me" is another externalization of a failure to learn schoolwork.

Once externalization of responsibility becomes a habit, then children and adolescents will have more difficulties in sustaining achievement behavior and responsibilities. Underachievement in such cases will become more and more a style of living. The longer such a style of living continues, the more likely it will become an ingrained part of the child's character and his fate as a human being, to the detriment of us all.

It is not possible to parent effectively without inflicting pain on children from time to time, but when I used the word "allow" in the context of "allowing a child to suffer," I mean the parent does not inflict the pain, the parent must insist that the child deal with his problems and his own inner self in response to achievement demands. The effective parent allows the pain to unfold so that the child can experience it. The effective parent does not go out of his way to create the suffering, or add even more pain. The effective parent waits patiently for opportunities to arise that allow him to bring to the light of his child's mind the potential that lies hidden in the darkness of irresponsibility, lies, clever excuses, and lack of self-discipline. When these opportunities arise, that is the time the effective parent goes out of his way to evoke the conscience of the child. It is the child's own conscience that causes him to feel guilt, low self-esteem, and emotional pain. When a child knows this, he can begin to heal himself.

Though suffering is an essential experience, the natural parental response to a suffering child should not be ignored or suppressed. In today's world, the word "love" is so often used to cover a multitude of sins and foibles that have nothing to do with love, that I'm afraid a whole book could be written about a parent's loving response to a suffering child before we could be clear what a loving response would be like. However, the word "compassion" may have more meaning. When a small child falls and cuts his knee, a compassionate parent comforts his child by acknowledging and examining the cut, and then administering healing medicine and soothing the anxiety.

Psychological pain is similar to physical pain, though the chief wounds are not of flesh and blood, but the loss of a personal sense of worth, discouragement, a sense of shame or guilt, feelings of incompetence, and anxiety about the future. A compassionate, loving parent acknowledges and helps his child examine the psychological pain with a soothing and comforting demeanor, while at the same time confronting the child to ensure he deals with his problems.

Being a soothing and comforting parent while at the same time being confrontational sounds to many like a contradiction in terms. Parents who are successful in containing this apparent contradiction and making it work for them follow what I've come to call the Ten Step Program. Parents who combine confrontation and the firm demands of discipline with compassion and understanding are more likely to secure the changes they want from their children.

Chapter 12

Disciplines for Change

The remainder of this book is devoted to the techniques of bringing about change in the way underachievers perform in their lives. The heart of these techniques is the Ten Step Program and Supplemental Disciplines that surround it to complete a new, disciplined approach to helping underachievers learn to motivate themselves to become successful. The purpose of these next chapters is to provide you, the parents, with a guide through the various techniques so that you can learn them in detail and follow them through the various twists and turns the paths to change normally follow in bringing underachieving children and adolescents to a new way of living for themselves.

Unfortunately, no manual or book can cover all the contingencies and versimilitudes involved in the causes and cures of underachievement—or any other chronic problem of the human heart. Parents may simply need to seek the help of experts if they are to be effective in changing their children's behavior and motivations.

The disciplines I am about to discuss are definitely designed to be both informative and thought-provoking. They are not just techniques to use carelessly. Any psychological or behavioral technique can be effective or ineffective depending on the attitude of the individual using the technique. A parent who is hostile may set limits on a child with disastrous results whereas the same parent who is compassionate may set the same limits on the same child with excellent results. There are no techniques to influence children's behaviors and motivations that have worked all the time. It is just that compassionate discipline works the best in the long run, far better than hostile discipline. Love makes the difference.

There are no guarantees of ultimate success. Not always is there treasure at the end of a journey toward positive change. Sadly, some paths lead nowhere but to heartaches. Parents' attempts to change their children's destiny is a good thing, even though the effort seems to be a failure for the time being. The question, you, as parents, must ask yourselves—"Is the effort worth it?" indeed, "Is your child worth it?"—if the results of effort cannot be predicted at the beginning of the journey? I can assure you that for most essentially normal children, positive change in their character and success orientation can be achieved through these methods, but each individual child is unique, and each child brings unique difficulties to the field of battle that may make the kind of positive changes in motivation and self-determined success problematically difficult at best.

Perhaps the best answer I can offer you is that the effort is worth it many times over. As parents, we want to be role models for our children. I have seen parents pull out all stops to engage in deep and persistent efforts over a long period of time to help their children make the positive changes that are the goals of this book. I have seen some kids show very few positive results for up to two years of effort. Yet, all the while, these difficult kids were learning something of value about the love and commitment of their parents for them, which eventually paid off in helping to develop solid, productive citizens later in life. Perhaps like the founding fathers of our country, we can win the war for freedom after losing most of the battles along the way. What parents need most in fighting this war for the hearts and minds of their children is a fundamental philosophy of parenting. This is the first Supplemental Discipline, developing a positive philosophy of parenting.

Supplemental Discipline I: a philosophy of parenting

We are all intertwined. As adults, we are the grown children of our parents. Even if they have passed away, and no matter how far we have journeyed from them, we are still bound to them in the emotional matrix and mythologies of our deepest selves. Even adopted children who have never known their biological parents still create half-conscious myths about them. By the same token, no matter how far they may journey beyond us, our children are bound to us and will be so even after we have passed away.

As parents, after a child is born to us we are never the same. Whether our children will bring us sadness and worry or joy and thanksgiving, we cannot tell at birth. Some children shatter us. Some bring us deep contentment. Mostly our children bring us a mixture of all of these feelings. Rearing children is complex and we cannot always know the consequences of our decisions regarding them until later. Much is unpredictable because they have their own brains, motivations, and emotions. What we can be absolutely sure of is that when the doctor cuts the umbilical cord at birth, an emotional umbilical cord is invisibly planted within us that attaches us to the destiny of our children forever. Over time, we gradually let them go. But no matter how far they stray from us, we always feel that invisible emotional bond, even if from a distance.

Between birth and that time where we must let them go on their own, our job as parents is to love them and train them to become the generation that must carry on after us. What legacy we leave them will largely be determined by what kind of parents we become as we grow with their developing minds and emotions. Our children always challenge us to grow beyond our own limitations if we are to do a good job with them. Often it is we who must change if we are to help them grow up. And it is often true that it is we who must finish growing up if we accept the true labor of parents and help our children become adults.

Over the years of helping parents and their children, I have had parents admonish me on many occasions. I warned them, they said, that their children could have a hard time and feel pain as part of their treatment. However, I failed to warn parents how difficult it could be for them as well. Yet, the growth in themselves and their children made it all worthwhile.

A crucial element in a proper philosophy of parenting deals with a special mental and emotional discipline. This discipline does not have a step by step procedure attached to it, for it is a discipline of the heart and must be learned. The discipline is deeply attitudinal, even spiritual, and it requires courage and commitment. Yet, it is such a part of everyday life that people often miss it completely, like a missing object we are desperately trying to find only to belatedly discover that it has been hidden in plain view all along.

The discipline of which I speak is one of radical responsibility. By "radical," I mean a sweeping feeling of being totally responsible for ourselves. So often parents take on the long task of parenthood with anxiety but also with joy and love. But what begins as excitement and joy, soon becomes a duty. Once a task becomes a duty, it soon becomes a burden we must carry. Our children are not responsible for our feelings as parents. We do not ask for children who have trouble. But they are our tasks and our responsibility to rear as best we can. To do this, we as parents must take on our tasks with all our might, to labor and work hard, putting our hearts and souls into our job. For there is nothing better a parent can do but to work at his or her parenting and to bring renewal, and joy, and love to that task no matter how challenging.

In essence, this technique is a discipline of renewal. When the heart wavers and feels tempted to give up, that is probably when our children need us the most, even if we are not sure how to be with them or just what to do to be effective and truly helpful. When parents want most to punish and condemn, that is when they need to recall their compassion. These are not easy tasks to do, nor even easy to place into words, for they are vital, living, growing abilities.

The best attitude a parent can assume throughout the various seasons of rearing children to adulthood is to see parenting as good, to see themselves as trying to create good. If parenting is innately good, then the major spiritual change in parents is to enjoy their lives as parents as much as possible because they will always be parents no matter what happens.

I have spent a large part of my professional life working with adolescents and children and parents from many races and nationalities. African-Americans, Hispanics, immigrants from Asia, people from Pakistan, India, Europe, South America, Greece, and Egypt. I have worked with the poor and the rich, those who came from privilege and those who would be considered underprivileged. The problems of underachievement know no cultural or racial boundaries. In all this work I have learned one overriding truth: Children who can feel love and participate in loving family relationships in which parents and children care for one another do better and learn how to work much more easily than when that love is blocked. I believe fundamentally that God gave us love first so that we could then go off and engage in the trials and effort involved in learning how to work and learn to love our work. Parents put their hearts in their children, then children put their hearts in their parents, and then children and adolescents separate from home and put their hearts into the work and tasks of their lives. In my experience, love comes first. It is primary. All psychological techniques and behavior-change technology are impotent if hate, resentment, and power replace love in the family relationships. As long as there is love, there is hope.

Love, then, is the fundamental philosophical problem of parenting. Parents must learn how to express their love when they use the Ten Step Program and the other Supplemental Disciplines that follow. They must express the love that is firm and kind, the love that binds, and the love that unbinds, the love that gives both discipline and freedom, and the love that can hold and that can let go. This is no small task and pain is so often a part of it. But as parents, that is what we signed up for when we decided to have our children. Their birth, or their adoption, was only our down payment. It is, after all, a great honor to be a parent who loves, and a great challenge.

I believe there is nothing better for a parent to do than to make their hearts enjoy the good that is in their parenting. If their children turn out well, then they will rejoice and will have already felt good throughout their efforts. If their children remain lost and troubled, then at least the parents will have done the absolute best they could have done under the circumstances. In their own hearts they will have experienced the good that was in their efforts and in their love. As long as parents can maintain commitment and love in their work of parenting, then there is hope that even the most wayward of children will someday see the light and discover within themselves the potential for enjoying the labor that lies within them like an eternal sunrise over the rim of their futures. Parents who can renew the joy of labor within themselves become emotional models for their children and can, by example, help their lost children learn to open their eyes and behold the eternal sun within.

Supplemental Discipline II: establishing the Totally Positive Parent approach

Whenever I am teaching parents how to bring motivation to their children, either as a psychotherapist or as a workshop leader, I try to instill in them what it means emotionally to become a positive parent. Being a positive parent goes beyond techniques or behavior strategies a parent might use to help their kids. Rather, being positive lies in the heart of the parents, in the emotions, attitudes and sense of faith and respect a parent brings to the trials and tribulations of rearing children who have their own hidden ways of seeing and feeling the world around them. Being a positive parent is much more than being a little Mr. or Mrs. Sunshine under all times and circumstances. It is certainly not being wimpy, flimsy, helpless, hapless, and spineless. Rather, a positive parent knows that children are works of art that take time and a lot of patience to create. They are works of art that have to be nurtured into creation, not driven or made by power oriented and angry demands. Positive parents know deep down within themselves that their children are works of art that ultimately must be self-creating, self-disciplining, and must learn to be self-motivating.

Most parents in the workshops or treatment sessions can acknowledge the attributes of a positive parent I have partially enumerated above, but they still need a way to revitalize the loving part of their parenting when they face troubles with their underachieving or misbehaving children. They need positive parenting attributes and attitudes most when they have to become firm and disciplined with their children.

Early in my training as a psychologist, I learned that if a person wants to change something about himself, one powerful way to do this is to create a vivid mental image of how one would behave. The powerful and vivid mental image, when evoked in the mind of the person under stress, changes the way that person behaves and feels, and this alters in positive ways the experience of stress.

All of us create mental images, anyway. Sometimes those mental images hurt us, sometimes they help us. I once treated a young woman with a severe phobia about speaking in public. Because she wanted to become a lawyer, her phobia was quite debilitating to her. Whenever she tried to speak before a class or an audience, she would become so panicked that she could not move or force herself to speak.

After several treatment sessions, she revealed a vivid mental image that accompanied her severe anxiety. She imagined that if she started speaking, she would become so nauseated that she would throw up on herself and then everyone would ridicule her. Her embarrassment and humiliation would prevent her from ever attending classes or being seen by members of the audience again. By taking control and changing that catastrophic mental imagery and replacing it with different imagery, she was able to eventually overcome her phobia of public speaking.

When parents confront their children's misbehavior and underachievement symptoms, they usually have negative mental imagery, negative emotions, and the situation with their own child becomes even more negative and tense. No one is happy. There is little productive change. One of the first changes parents make (and remember, it is almost always the parents who must change before their children can change) is that they create for themselves a vividly positive mental image that alters their attitudes and emotions in dealing with the stress of their children's self-defeating and sometimes obnoxious behavior.

But what kind of image can parents create that is effective? When I ask parents that very question, I rarely get a good mental image as a response. The contents of the mind are too vague. Sometimes I get answers like, "I tell myself to remain calm and smile." "I count from ten backward before I talk."

These and other things parents tell themselves are like self-instructions. Giving oneself instructions is good, but I am looking for that positive mental image that is so vivid that it alone begins to change feelings and behavior. Because I usually have to suggest an image to most people to teach them the idea I have in mind, I will assume that you, the reader, need a suggestion from me as well.

I want all the readers of this text to follow my directions carefully and faithfully. I want you to watch television, PBS television to be exact. I want you to use your VCR if you have to, but I want you to watch *Mr. Rogers' Neighborhood.* I want you to watch him sing his song "Welcome to My Neighborhood." I want you to study his mannerisms and his style, his calm, his respect, his focus, his movements, and his kindness. I want you to watch him more than once, but at least six times *all the way through his show!* Then, whenever you have to deal with your child's misbehavior or underachievement symptoms (e.g., poor report cards, lying about homework, trouble in school), I want you to confront your child and lay down discipline just like Mr. Rogers would do.

Whenever I bring up Mr. Rogers in a seminar, I get two reactions from the audience. About half the audience smiles and nods in recognition and approval and about half start shaking their heads, "No!" The no crowd say they cannot stand Mr. Rogers. I then tell them about Mr. James, whom I worked with in the early years of my practice with underachievers.

Mr. James (which is not his real name) was a high school dropout who worked hard in physical labor so that he could put his son through college. He was bound and determined that his son would not make the same mistakes he had made.

Unfortunately, Mr. James's son had failed the ninth grade already and was in the process of failing it once more. This father had never physically hurt his son, but was a hard and rough man and used tough discipline. His wife was more lenient.

In treatment, very little was working, and I was searching for a way to reach Mr. James to help him deal differently with his son. I suggested that he watch Mr. Rogers. Mr. James, at first, had a typically negative reaction to Mr. Rogers: he hated him. But since I was the doctor, he watched the program faithfully for two weeks so he could develop the proper mental image. While this was going on, I observed that he and his wife grew closer together as parents. He became softer in dealing with his son, and she became a little harder. This was a good change.

We rehearsed the totally positive parent approach because report card time was upon this family once more and John (the son) was likely to fail once more. This is how the parents handled the report card day.

Both parents walked into their son's room—holding hands—and asked to see his report card. At first John maintained he had not received his card, but Mom found it later in his blue jeans pocket when she was doing the laundry. They walked back into John's room—holding hands—to confront John about his grades. Mr. James, all six foot three inches of him, unfolded the card and studied it in front of his son. John had managed to fail every subject, including physical education classes, except history. He had made a C in history. Dad and Mom gave their son a hug and Dad said, in his best "Mr. Rogers" style, "I'm so glad you enjoyed history more this time." Then he left the room.

In preparation for this moment, I told the father that when they left John, he would probably follow them around the house. The father actually timed his son, who took just about twelve seconds to leave his room and come to his parents, who were sitting in the den.

John stood before his parents. He had a confused and surprised look on his face. "But, Dad," he said, "what about these Fs? Did you see these?"

Now, this was the second real change in John. The first change was being bewildered over his parents' reaction and following them around the house. The second change was that it was now he who was pointing out his bad grades, not his parents. This is how underachievers begin to change—in small but important ways.

The father continued his totally positive parenting approach. He looked at the report card and said, "Yes, son, I see those Fs. But you know, they are high Fs. It takes some effort and learning to make a 65 in math and a 59 in English. And what is more important, anyway, making grades or learning? If you just keep trying and just keep learning, you will eventually learn to be successful, like you were in history. Your mother and I will help you."

As time wore on, early elements of the Ten Step Program were used and excuse after excuse became unhooked and John's grades began to rise a little. He was no longer failing but was not reaching his considerable potential either. The father continued to be positive throughout. The father's positive emotional and behavioral change became the most critical element in his son's treatment.

John had superior intellectual ability. But he knew his father's struggles and his father's school history. John knew his father's dreams for his son. And John felt a hidden pain. One evening in a treatment session, tears came to John's eyes as his father and I were focusing on John's thoughts and feelings about his failure to turn in several important assignments leading to significant failures in two classes. John looked pleadingly at his father and said that no one really understood anything. "I can't do well in school, Dad. I just can't," he said. When gently pressed for an explanation by his father, John replied, "I love you, Dad. I just can't become more than you."

The core causes of children's underachievement are always unique and more often than not, surprising. John certainly surprised me, his father, and, truly, even himself. John was motivated to fail the ninth grade so he would not surpass his beloved father, the father whose self-esteem he was unconsciously protecting by failing. John was eventually able to tell his father his deepest fears and feelings only because his father had the courage to change his demanding anger into love, respect, and true listening.

As a psychologist, it is still amazing to me how quickly most children change once they and their parents realize the core motivations that drive them to fail. It is not magic. It is that parents and children can now deal with reality and understanding. There are subtle but powerful emotional and behavioral shifts as the family accommodates to these motivational realities, and then develops new ones. John went on to fulfill his own and his father's dreams. He went to college and graduated. More important, Mr. James gave his son the gift of a loving, understanding father, and John gave his father the gift of a successful son.

Becoming a Totally Positive Parent is an ideal for which parents should strive. No parents are perfect. There will be many moments in helping chronic underachievers change their lives that parents will be stumped and bewildered as to how to respond to things their children do or say, and plenty of times the parents will express negative feelings about their children's attitudes and behavior. However, the closer parents become to being Totally Positive Parents who express love, compassion, understanding, and mercy while also being disciplined and firm, the more they will be the parents who can quickly recover from negative feelings to reestablish positive relationships with their children. Parents who actively work for the Totally Positive Parent ideal will likely be more successful in changing their children than the parents who remain locked into negative feelings, attitudes, and the pushing, punitive, power-oriented relationships with their underachievers.

The Totally Positive Parent is an ideal that was created out of my work with parents as a foil to the negativity that always happens in the families who try to cope with underachievers. I have found a great deal of tension in the families of underachievers, especially during the stresses and strains of a school year. The parents are usually angry, frustrated, and punitive. Underachievers are irresponsible, rebellious, and passive. As the school year progresses, the tensions increase because things do not get better. They either stay the same or just get worse. Nothing seems to help.

The negativity between parents and children can be seen in the simplest moments. For example, Johnny comes home from school and walks in the door of his home. His mother greets him and asks how school was. She wants information about his day because Johnny is not doing well. However, Johnny does not give her any information. All he says is, "Fine." She knows that if she does not ask more questions, that is all she will ever hear. So the tensions begin. Mom must ask twenty questions just to get a straight answer, and Johnny resents the questions. He would rather leave things vague and not give specific answers. If he leaves things vague, he can get out of doing things he does not want to do. There is no cooperation between parent and child, there is only opposition and maneuver.

To continue the moment a little longer, typically, Mom asks if Johnny has any homework. Now things get even worse. Johnny tells her, "No, I did it all at school."

Mom thinks, "Is he lying?" After all, he has lied or "forgotten" his homework before. She knows she is not getting the truth, so when he goes outside to play with his friends, or she finds him on the phone excessively, she resents and doubts him even more. This scene and scenes like this are repeated in homes all across America, and in the few moments this interaction takes is revealed only a bit of the tensions, mistrust, lack of communication, and pain of the underachievement lifestyle. We have not yet even dealt with actually making sure the homework is done or finding out grades.

Totally Positive Parents must develop certain attributes that help things remain positive even in trying circumstances. Some of these attributes are listed below. As an aspiring Totally Positive Parent, you:

1. Assume full responsibility for training your child to meet the demands of adulthood. You must rear your child so that he has the best chance to make a significant contribution to others and to become a satisfied, happy individual who can love others, love himself, and have a strong capacity to work and enjoy his labor.

2. You must help your child gain the insight he needs to take control of himself, make commitments, have courage, and develop a better, positive relationship with you. You cannot teach your child to have insight into himself if you constantly make excuses for your own poor behavior. It is absolutely essential for you to try to become a better person yourself.

3. You must understand it is you, not your child, who will change first. You must understand that you have somehow, even if inadvertently, fed your child's problems; even caused some of them. You, then, must change your ways before your child can or will change. This change includes seeking help when your efforts are not working. An underachiever never seeks advice when he needs it, so you do not become an underachiever as a parent. If you need help, find it. Reading this book helps, but no book, not even mine, can answer your individual questions if you feel stuck in a problem you cannot solve.

4. You must not be afraid of making mistakes. Most parents, even those making Herculean efforts to remain positive, will get negative from time to time. So what? Get back on the positive track as soon as you can. Nothing helps a child learn respect for important relationships more than when a parent apologizes for inappropriate behavior and begins to change. When you make a mistake, be man or woman enough to own up to it and begin correcting it.

5. You must at all times remember that your adolescent child is emotionally equal to you. You, however, are probably superior in life experience and in judgment. You may be generally superior in emotional development and control, moral development, capacity for empathy, and in the ability to engage in complex adaptive thinking and behavior demanded of adults. However, if you saw the world as your child sees it, if you felt about things as he does, if you had his ideas and attitudes, then you would do the exact same things he does. If you remember only this one truth, that your child is emotionally your peer, then you may help yourself become a more positive parent during times of stress. At least you will never talk down to your child or underestimate him or the importance of understanding his heart and mind if you are to help him really change. The strategy of being a Totally Positive Parent is an important cornerstone of the Ten Step Program discussed later in this book. It is important to be positive parents because all underachievers are discouraged children who hide their feelings of discouragement, their pain of shame and guilt, and their fears of the future through their excuses and irresponsibility. For most underachievers, turning around their lives means they will have to more openly experience the very emotions they have been hiding away from themselves and from others. In other words, they may feel more negative and anxious for a while before they learn to feel better. Underachievers will not allow parents or any other adults to help them if their relationships with adults are painful. They will not allow themselves to feel their own self-caused pain if they also have to feel the pain others inflict upon them. Further, as informed parents, you must hear and understand your children's inner thoughts and feelings and the conflicts they have with themselves. They will not give you their hearts and minds as long as they are afraid they will be punished somehow when they do so. They will not only continue to hide from you, but will also continue to hide from themselves. Positive parents help their children learn how to know themselves and learn how to become emotionally closer to their parents. The growth of closeness and self-knowledge allows children to change.

Becoming a Totally Positive Parent allows parents the opportunity to become the stewards of their children's growth to adulthood, not their jailers. Often, parents must first change the character of their own behavior and attitudes toward the underachievers before the underachievers are ready to make the necessary changes. As stewards, parents must come to value the virtues of stewardship: compassion for their children's struggles; richness in their feelings and communication with their children; and emotional closeness and kindness in the discipline of their children. These form the foundation for their children's successes and love of work later in life. The parents' stewardship virtues allow their children to learn, grow, and find heart and meaning in life because their children are reared by parents who in turn learn, grow, and find heart and meaning in the parenting of their children.

As critical and as helpful as developing a more positive approach can be, most underachievers will need more than positive parenting alone to help them overcome their long-standing problems. However, the parents may have contributed to their children's problems in the past, and however much they change, most underachievers have internalized their problems. Self-defeating patterns of behavior are now functionally autonomous from the parents. That is, changing the environment or parenting patterns will not likely by themselves change the self-defeating patterns of underachievement. Underachievers actualize their problems in their attitudes, feelings, self-concepts, and in their behavior. Therefore, real and lasting change must come from within the underachiever.

Good-natured caring plus discipline based on understanding is missing from many families with underachievers. Positive parents who have compassion and understanding can create good, loving discipline, which produces gratitude in our children. This is the kind of discipline underachievers need, not the cold demands, the inconsistencies, and the overprotectiveness sometimes found in the homes of underachievers. Children need discipline and a relationship with parents wherein they learn courage, commitment, compassion, and steadiness in a changing world; a discipline where children learn how to pursue life from the heart outward, to accept responsibility, and to make sacrifices for worthwhile goals. As stewards to the next generation of American citizens, is Positive Parenting and firm and loving discipline not a good heritage for our children and our children's children who will carry on after them?

Supplemental Discipline III: ending lying about school.

In anticipation of following the steps of the Ten Step Program, most underachievers will have trouble giving parents the information about school that is needed for parents to help them. The giving of information is a rational response, but underachievers are not rational when it comes to school. In fact, they lie often and hide the truth about their work when they do not actually lie. Therefore, the first major battle to be fought between parents and children will reside in being honest and telling the truth about schoolwork.

The fact that kids lie, however, does in no way damage the power of the Ten Step Program in helping change underachievers. As a matter of fact, as discussed later on, the Ten Step Program is equally useful in confronting lying behavior as well as decisions to sabotage success.

Most underachievers lie about school because they believe that if they mess up, being honest about it will only lead them to feel worse. They believe their parents will not react positively, but will react negatively with punishment, shaming, or some other harsh reaction. Children themselves are very creative imaginatively and can think of many other reasons for hiding the truth about their activities from their parents. Regardless of the reasons for dishonesty, just asking for honesty is not enough to change children's lying. Their dishonesty and its destructive consequences for the child himself and his family must be confronted.

The first step in setting up a proper confrontation over a child's dishonesty and lack of trustworthiness is for the parent to set up the proper conditions under which a child's honesty can be gently tested. The following are components of proper conditions for testing honesty.

ATTITUDE: The parents will assume a totally positive attitude when their child fails the test. The idea is not to punish, but to understand and help their child change.

CONDITIONS: The parents will tell their child in Step 1 of the Ten Step Program that they want only to help him get what he really wants in school. They announce that they really want him to do things his way, all they want to know is how his way is working, and if it is not working, then what he will do about it.

WHAT THE CHILD DOES: The child will come home from school every day and give one or both parents a report about what happened in school. Hopefully, the parents will not have to ask any questions, but the child's report should include information about each class. Parents may take notes. In each class, the child will recount briefly what he studied in class, what homework was assigned, if any grades were handed back or given that day, if he had any missing assignments (any zeros), what tests are coming up, and any long-term projects. If the child announces an upcoming test, then the parent asks what grade he wants to make on that test. If the child says he failed to turn in homework, the parent asks how that happened and simply notes the excuses. At the end of the report, the parent asks the child when he plans on doing his homework or plans on studying that night, if he has not already done these things. Then the parent asks if his child needs any help, and then plans out that help only if his child asks for it.

WHAT THE PARENTS DO: The parents tell their child to confess the full story about school to them, the good, the bad, and the ugly. They promise not to become angry, agitated, blaming, disappointed, or even overly frustrated. They will not ground, spank, blame, or in any way punish their child for setbacks, slipups, poor grades, or failures. They do promise, however, to try to understand what happened to create slipups and help their child come up with concrete plans to overcome those problems. The parents should use all or selected parts of the Ten Step Program to help a child understand how failures occurred and make plans to handle them next time.

The aim here is to gain a consensual commitment from their child to report honestly about school. At the very least, parents will assertively and strongly tell their child that they expect honesty and truth when he tells them about school.

Do not simply rely on a child's commitment to veracity, no matter how sincerely made. The parents' job in this technique is to find out the truth. The parents will call the school at the end of the first week or two of this plan and check with the teachers on three issues: does their child have any missing work (zeros), any grades D or below, and any other problems with missing or late work? This is usually where parents find out their child has not been entirely forthcoming about his progress and behavior in school. The parents discover deceit and dishonesty.

WHAT PARENTS DO NOW: Parents always remain calm and patiently wait for the best opportunity for confronting their child's dishonesty. The problem with lying and deceitfulness, no matter how understandable such behavior may be from the child's point of view, is that such behavior tears at the fabric of the trust relationships between children and parents. A very good case can be made that for children to develop their own independent sense of identity, they must keep some secrets from their parents. However, school is not a privacy issue. It does harm to underachievers when they continue to lie and deceive about their problems.

Parents choose their time well, such as when their child asks to go somewhere during the weekend. The parents should be calm and listen well to their child's requests to do something with friends, for example. The parents should appear eager to respond positively to their child's request. There is just one thing they need to bring up. Then, the parents tell their child that they are not quite sure what their child means when he says things to them because they called his teachers recently and discovered that he had withheld information, or maybe he had even lied to the parents about school. There are now two problems to resolve. One is that his grades are lower than his goals, and they need to discuss the issue thoroughly. Two is that he is lying to them and they do not know why, or if they can fully trust him. Only when trust is reestablished and difficulties with school dealt with can he go out and play during his free time. Until then, he needs to stick near his parents so he can discuss what is going on.

If the child asks, "How long will this take?" the parents should respond with something like: "I don't know how long it will take you to reestablish trust so that we can believe what you say, and I don't know how long it will take you to deal thoroughly with the problems in school. We can begin discussing these things anytime you wish. It may take all weekend and the next few. But whenever you have settled these things, of course you can have free time with your friends."

If the child asks, "Am I grounded?" say, "No." You don't believe in grounding. What you do believe in is honesty and in his establishing and living out a different relationship with you.

At this point, cycle through the appropriate steps of the Ten Step Program on both issues: the lying and the failures in school. Continue to cycle through this technique until your child's behavior begins to change with the confrontations and Ten Step Program. Remember, the Ten Step Program is a problem solving program that makes the child responsible for solving problems he creates for himself and for others. It can be used for many different kinds of behaviors and problems, not just for grades.

Supplemental Discipline IV: establishing the "Work Must Be Done" policy

Before completing Step 1 of the Ten Step Program, parents can establish this work policy, especially when one of the signs of underachievement is a child's passive refusals to do homework. Essentially, the parents discuss the need for their child to gradually learn how to be an adult in life, and school is his training ground for learning to handle work. Homework is his assigned task. In the adult world, no one ordinarily gets out of doing work just because they do not do it one day. They simply have to do it the next day. Further, parents explain that learning how to do work is a vital value, and very important to them personally. They would be very irresponsible as parents to not train him how to work as an adult.

The parents announce that they understand that their child has his own goals to do better in school. They then ask their child to calculate how many 100s it takes to bring one zero up to the lowest B. Children and adolescents almost always underestimate the impact a zero has on the mean score. This is done so that the child thoroughly understands the impact of very low scores on grade averages.

Next, the parents say that if the child wants to sabotage his grades by not doing work and getting zeros, then they will want to know his motive for doing so and help him with those self-defeating motivations. However, all missing work must be done even if a teacher refuses to accept the missing work and the child gets no credit. In this way, the value of finishing assigned tasks is reinforced and the child is taught that work must be completed. Since one of the persistent problems of most under-achievers is that they do not finish or even do homework, then this technique directly counters that propensity. Furthermore, many underachievers believe that it is no big deal when they do not do homework. They feel that one zero will not affect them, and magically, when they do not do work, their undone work does not pile up like in the adult world, it just disappears and they are never called on to finish it. Making them finish undone work simply demands of children the same standards they will have to face as adults. It trains them to become mature and responsible.

If the child comes home and, during the school report time, says he got a zero in math because he "forgot" to do an assignment, then the "forgetting" is handled through the Ten Step Program. The missing work, however, must be done. The child may do it and show the parents during the week, or he may choose to do it on the weekends on his own time. However, the missing work must be completed *before* he can do *anything* else on the weekend. In essence, the child grounds himself to his parents until his work is done. If his parents want him to go someplace or do something that is good for him to do, such as go to Sunday school or church, then he must do those activities, but he has no free time until all his missing work is done.

If a child has lied about his zeros and the parents find out about it, they confront him on the weekend, just like in the previous supplemental discipline, *Ending Lying About School.* However, in this technique, he does his work before any play. No television, or computer games, no telephone calls, no friends, and no leisure pursuits. If the child says he forgot and left his books or papers at school and cannot, therefore, do his assignments, then his parents can be very sympathetic, but not having the proper materials to complete his task is *his* problem to solve, not *theirs.* The parents will be glad to allow him to sit at the kitchen table all weekend if necessary, even if he cannot do his work, until he solves the problem. The parents should use elements of the Ten Step Program to help him solve the problem. Once there is a solution focus, it is amazing how often underachievers begin to come up with solutions, including never letting themselves forget homework again. When most kids understand that their parents are absolutely serious about the "work first" policy, many will start doing their work.

It is imperative that the child know about this plan in advance if it is to be effective. Few underachievers will respond well at first because they truly believe that if they whine and complain that they are helpless and how "unfair" the parents are acting, then they will get out of work once more. By knowing the consequences in advance, children learn they invite the consequences by not doing work or by lying. They demonstrate that it is they who have the problem, not their parents or anyone else.

There are some kids who are so self-defeating, depressed, rebellious, or angry, that they continue not to do homework despite parental consistency on the "work must be done" rule. After several weeks of persistent, self-defeating behavior, a consultation with a professional familiar with chronic motivational problems is recommended to help resolve the causes of this level of problem.

Supplemental Discipline V: no grades below a C

This is a relatively straightforward discipline often used in conjunction with the two techniques discussed above. This is often used with severe underachievement problems or when kids have failed courses or grades. Sometimes, after using the Ten Step Program for a grading period or two, the underachiever's changes in study behavior are too erratic or slow to keep him from failing. This discipline is useful in that situation as well.

At the same point in Step 1 of the Ten Step Program, the parents modify the Step 1 procedures and simply establish the need for extra study beyond the homework to prevent failure. The parents assert that Ds will require an extra hour of supervised study, either during the week or on the weekend. A grade of F in a subject will require an extra hour and a half of supervised study in that subject either during the week or on the weekend.

This technique is most effective when used with *Ending Lying About School* and *Work Must Be Done*. In other words, the child gives a daily school report. Only now, when he says he has grades below a C (and a zero on homework is both below a C and it also must be done, anyway), then he has to create a schedule for his extra study time in addition to having to go through the steps for problem solving in the Ten Step Program.

Supplemental Discipline VI: encountering resistance and dependency—who's the boss?

This is not so much a technique as it is an issue interwoven throughout the use of the Ten Step Program and these supplemental disciplines. Almost every underachiever will continue to show problems with follow-through, will resist efforts to help him, and will evidence dependency when he has to be supervised or dealt with in some way in areas of life where he needs to be independent, such as school. When parents employ the Ten Step Program and the supplemental techniques, there almost always comes a time when a child resists rational advances in his work, even when he wants to do well. When he cannot come up with reasonable plans; when he cannot follow through on his own plans; when he continues to lie and hide his grades and homework; when he continues to rebel actively or passively and cling to irrational and self-defeating behavior and attitudes, then the parents must bring up the dependency issue that underlies his failures. This is the problem of who is going to be the child's boss, himself or his parents?

WHAT PARENTS DO AND SAY: When parents raise this issue, they do so calmly so that the child has to focus on their words and not their anger or threats. The parents must verbally reaffirm their commitment to their child's autonomy and independence. However, if he cannot make himself follow through with a plan or even make one, then he is literally telling them, with his behavior, that he is not mature and independent enough to be his own boss, exercise authority over himself, and show enough self-discipline to make himself do the right thing. The parents assert that if their child needs a boss, they will step in and be his boss. However, and this must be very clear, they will not be able to lead him his way, because his way fails. If he needs them to take over and be his boss, he will have to work the way they would work if they were in his circumstances. In other words, if he cannot exercise enough self-control and self-direction to follow his own plans or make them, then his behavior is asking for a boss and he can do things their way until he learns their way thoroughly enough. Then he can try things his way again when he has learned from his parents.

As an example, one young man had continued to lie about his grades and withhold information from his parents about school. He had several major tests announced for the following week, when his father confronted his son's rebellious and secretly dependent behavior. The parents had called the school and found out their son's grades and about the upcoming examinations. The father then confronted his son about his lying, the lack of trust, the grades, and his son's dependency behavior. He told his son that he would observe him over a period of a few days. If his son's behavior continued to demonstrate his dependency and inability to work, then his father would take over and his son would study the father's way—the way his father would study if he were in his son's shoes. The father then explained how he would study all weekend until he knew the material for the examinations.

By Friday, his son had continued to show procrastination and refusal to make concrete plans for studying and learning. On Friday evening his father took charge. By that time, even this recalcitrant young man had to acknowledge that he was unable to be his own boss. He complied with his father's study schedule and submitted to his father's benevolent but firm direction. He did well on his exams. About two weeks after initiating close supervision, the father was able to gradually return autonomy to his son by using the Ten Step Program.

CONFRONTING DECISIONS TO SEEK DEPENDENCY: When parents take their child through the Ten Step Program, they will isolate moments when their child has made a decision that became a turning point and the consequences of that decision led to a failure. When this happens over and over again, the child is consciously seeking dependency. By isolating these decision points, the parents begin to reinterpret their child's decision as not only decisions to fail, but also as decisions to make themselves dependent of the parents' supervision. Once this reinterpretation is made, the parents institute reviews of the decisions their child makes to become independent and decisions he makes to be irresponsible and, thus, to make himself dependent on his parents.

Under this regimen of decision analysis, children and adolescents who continue to make dependent and irresponsible decisions may be communicating that they are too emotionally immature to have the freedoms usual for individuals their age.

For example, do parents allow a dependency-seeking irresponsible adolescent to drive a car with which he could injure himself or others?

Supplemental Discipline VII: the Socratic dialogue technique

Socrates was a master teacher. Socrates believed fervently that one could find truth and wisdom by simply asking good questions that required respondents to give specific and concrete answers. In one of the dialogues of Plato, Socrates taught a young student geometry not by lecturing or through demonstrations, but by asking detailed questions that led the boy step by step to knowledge of geometric concepts. The Socratic Method, as it came to be known, is a technique used often by psychotherapists, lawyers, U.S. Senate investigating committees, and by some parents.

I give my mother and father credit for introducing me to a modern version of the Socratic Method employed by the television character Columbo. Columbo always had one more good question to ask that required a specific, concrete answer. No one answer in itself was enough to hang the bad guy, but by asking such seemingly ridiculous and overly detailed questions, Columbo was able to piece together a coherent picture of events and in so doing, he caught the thief every time. Parents are encouraged to use the "Columbo" or Socratic Method extensively in the Ten Step Program. In fact, its use is *required*. The Socratic Method allows parents an escape from dictating answers to dilemmas and problems that should properly come from the kids themselves. By using the Socratic Method, the underachievers will be placed in the responsible position of having to generate their own thoughts and solutions to their own problems. They will not like this, which is why I have chosen the character Columbo for parents to pattern after. When people got mad at him for asking them one more "stupid" question, he simply remained calm and insistent on specificity. That is the watchword for the Ten Step Program: *specify, specify, specify.* Let nothing vague go unexplained. Leave no stones unturned. Eventually, excuses will be shattered, answers will be found, and understanding will eventually grow. The use of the Socratic dialogue technique will become clearer as the Ten Step Program is presented in the next two chapters.

Part II

The Solution

Introduction to the Ten Step Program

Chapters 13 and 14 are devoted to the Ten Step Program, a technique and discipline that is the heart and soul of changing the character patterns of underachievers and helping them become independent and successful individuals. Without the Ten Step Program, the supplemental disciplines discussed in the previous chapter, indeed, most educational and skill training remedies for underachievement, are likely to prove insufficient.

The Ten Step Program is a series of steps parents follow that eventually reveals what is hidden in children's minds that leads them to fail their potential and seem lazy and disinterested in success and their own future. It is a series of steps that leads down to the causes of failure and leads back up to solving those problems and helping kids make new decisions that unlock their potential and help them learn how to motivate themselves. By going through these steps, children can learn to understand themselves, think out their own solutions to their problems, exercise self-discipline, and learn to feel positive feelings about schoolwork. The program helps children learn to direct their behavior, attitudes, and feelings toward the fulfill-ment of goals that are in their own best interests and, if neces-sary, sacrifice of the pleasures and escapes of the moment to achieve their long-term goals and gains. These steps will also help most youngsters learn to confront and defeat perfec-tionism, procrastination, overcome discouragement, mild to moderate depressions associated with underachievement, help them learn to regulate self-esteem, and build their own self-confidence.

By faithfully and consistently following the Ten Step Pro-gram, parents may lead their underachieving children to a greater awareness of the difference between what they say they want and what they do on a daily basis to sabotage their goals. Children are led by their own plans to see how inconsistent they are, how they stop working and fail, and what feelings and attitudes are involved in their underachievement. They are brought slowly to believe they are responsible for changing themselves. Often, they are even led to see that they want con-flicting things, and they will finally have to make up their minds as to what they stand for in life.

In other words, the Ten Step Program leads underachievers to a crossroad in their lives where they have to make conscious and clear decisions either to fail or to succeed. By being brought to these crossroads where a decision must be made, they are stripped of excuses for failures. If success or failure flows from a decision one must make, then only the person making that decision can be responsible for it. Bringing underachievers to a crossroad allows them to become empowered and responsible and to gain the pride and self-respect that springs from assum-ing responsibility and making one's own way in life.

There are basically two stages to the Ten Step Program. The first stage is covered by Steps 1 through 5 in Chapter 13. Chapter 13 sets the stage for the deeper changes to occur in Steps 6 through 10 covered in Chapter 14. The steps in Chapter 14 are key ingredients to helping your child create lasting positive changes in work ethic and motivation.

It is important to read both Chapters 13 and 14 to grasp the full picture of how it all works. I have provided case examples that will allow you to gain a thorough grasp of the principles and issues involved in each step and to see how they fit together to provide a comprehensive responsibility-and-motivation-creating program for good kids with chronic underachievement problems.

Let me offer one more word before you read on and begin to apply the Ten Step Program. I want to stress that this is a repetitive, consistent, firm, and long-term approach to the problem of underachievement. This should be good news to most of you reading this, for you have already used most of the quick fix approaches and have seen them fail. It is time for a long-term solution to this thorny problem.

Let me be as encouraging to you as I can. I have found that the more this approach is used, the more effective it becomes. However, you must expect progress and setbacks. Celebrate the progress and keep working patiently on the setbacks. The process is a kind of training to get your children to internalize the Ten Step Program for themselves as they learn how to enjoy a strong work ethic. You, as parents, will know that your persistence, commitment, and repetition of the steps in the following chapters are paying off, not just when your child starts making better grades on his own, but more deeply, when you see him begin to think for himself, come up with solutions for his own problems, and work to fix those problems. In other words, you know he is getting better when he starts to use the Ten Step Program on himself and unhooks himself from his own excuses.

Chapter 13

Setting the Stage

Before continuing to read this book, please take about ten minutes and commit the following ten steps to memory. See if you can anticipate what these steps are all about before I discuss them.

Step 1: Establish values of honesty, trust, and truth.

Step 2: Set long-term and short-term goals.

Step 3: Explore how goals will be achieved.

Step 4: Select one problem and explore your child's perspective.

Step 5: Link your child's problem to goal attainment or failure.

Step 6: Help your child make concrete plans to solve achievement problems.

Step 7: Redefine success and failure as following his own plans—analyze the decisions he must make to succeed or fail.

Step 8: Initiate introspection—explore conflicts and feelings about following his plans.

Step 9: Cement commitments to follow through on plans.

Step 10: Perform follow-up and a sequence analysis of his specific decisions to succeed or fail.

Step 1: Establish values of honesty, trust, and truth.

Trust is a crucial value in the health and vitality of a family, and there can be no trust between parents and children when parents cannot believe the words their children tell them. Underachievers rarely report honestly the facts about their academic progress to their parents, thus breaking the trust bonds between parents and children. The motivations behind these almost daily deceptions are varied, but most of the time children lie about school to protect themselves from the consequences their parents often lay on them. The objective of this step is to fundamentally alter the family dynamics of lying and deception about schoolwork so that the trust bond between parents and their children may be reestablished. Once children no longer lie about schoolwork, they are much more likely to become reconnected with the success values and conscience that lies hidden inside of them. In other words, they will gradually become exposed to the inner consequences of laziness, failure, and lack of follow-through, which is a much more powerful motivator for positive change than anything you could ever do to them from the outside.

Probably the best way of initiating conversation about honesty and trust regarding school is to simply ask your child for the truth. It is important to acknowledge that your child has deceived or inaccurately reported the facts about schoolwork to you previously. You can even acknowledge that you may have inadvertently contributed to deception by becoming angry or punishing whenever you learned of poor grades or missing work in the past.

Announce to your child that you want to change the way things work between the two of you. You want your child to tell you all the good and bad facts about his schoolwork and grades on a daily basis. You want to know about each class, what he did in that class, if he turned in all his work or not, if he has tests or quizzes coming up, what grades he wants to make on those tests; you want to know about projects, when they are due, and what grades he wants to make on them; and you want to know each day what grades he has gotten back in each class. You will sit down and have a brief conversation with him daily about each of these questions, and you will even keep notes or a chart of his answers. During this daily conversation, you want only the truth about work and grades. Tell him that continuing to deceive or lie to you about school is a serious matter and will likely require that he spend many weekends bonding with you and discussing his motivations and need for change. It is always easier to deal with schoolwork than to deal with the thorny problems presented by having to rebuild trust.

Tell your child that he will be able to trust you. You pledge to him that you will no longer ground, lecture, yell, scream, punish, bribe with privileges, or pay him to get the grades you would like. Rather, you are simply going to help him learn how to help himself and succeed in his own way, without nagging or threats from you. You want him to learn to be his own boss in school, to be independent and motivated on his own, feel good about himself and his schoolwork, to work realistically on his own future and to someday achieve his dreams, and, above all, to solve his own problems while maintaining trust with you.

Tell him that you realize that Rome was not built in a day and that it will take some time for him to learn how to motivate himself, how to be independent in his work, to feel good about his work, and to learn to be his own boss in solving problems. Tell him that you may need to become more involved from time to time to train him how to do all these things for himself, but you promise to be patient and kind during those times when he gets stuck in his progress. In other words, if he fails continuously to follow through on his own plans and ideas to be more successful in school, he will be telling you that he is too dependent on you to be his own boss, and you may need to be his boss for a short time to train him to overcome whatever sticky problem that defeats him in getting what he wants. However, you cannot help him become independent and successful if he remains deceptive or dishonest about the simple facts of his academic life.

Finally, tell your child that he may slip up and the old patterns of underachievement and the old deceptiveness may return from time to time. No one is perfect and change can be slow and difficult at times. Tell him that failure or the reemergence of old problems are simply another opportunity to work through these problems and overcome them once and for all.

Complications:

Sometimes a student will respond negatively to the implication that he needs help in solving his school problems. Usually, this type of student will stress that he can handle things on his own, or that he does not want you involved or interfering with his way of doing things. "Quit nagging me and let me do it on my own" is the usual demand they make.

Actually, this is just the message most parents want to hear from their underachieving children. Unfortunately, most of the time, parents are right to doubt such promises to do better because unless specific behavior and attitudes change, the best predictor of future behavior is a child's past behavior.

Many discouraged children desire privacy when it comes to schoolwork and grades because hiding this area of life from view helps to protect them from emotional pain. After all, who in his right mind would want to expose his personal weaknesses to angry, judgmental, and overly critical people who add insult to injury through their anger, shaming lectures, and punishment? It will take a while for children to come to trust parents with their academic secrets.

As painful as it may be for a child, it is crucial that he learn to discuss openly his mistakes, failings, and his successes. School is not a privacy issue, no more than performance on the job is a matter of privacy for an employee at work. For an underachiever to change, what is hidden must be brought to the light of day in a caring and sensitive manner. This way, the child is gradually trained to become responsible and to live in the adult world, which he must inherit someday.

If your child stubbornly insists he can do well on his own and solve his own problems despite contrary evidence, it does no good to keep repeating all the broken promises of the past, even if that past is merely weeks old. Rather, you can align yourself with your child on this issue by agreeing it would be best if he were so independent as to require no help from you. However, you need to ask what role you should play in his newly found independence and should inquire if he wishes you to stay completely out of his schoolwork. If he wants you to be totally out, then you simply say that his idea is a good one, but it is not acceptable at this time due solely to his past performances. However, you will honor his request as much as you possibly can by remaining positive if he has problems and by letting him create his own solutions to whatever problems may emerge. Your only requirement is that he keeps you fully informed about what is going on. You will only ask him questions to clarify your understanding of what he is doing or plans to do to fix his problems. Then you reaffirm the need for trust and honesty.

Your child may be resistant, even hostile and obstinate, to this approach initially. Remain firm and committed. The vast majority of children and teenagers will come around. However, if his hostility and resistance remains high and troublesome for more than a couple of weeks and you cannot even get past Step 1 (or Step 2 below), then you will likely need the outside assistance of a psychologist or family oriented therapist to help you reach a cooperative relationship with your child. Rational and mature individuals always seek help when they need it.

The philosophy of the Ten Step Program is really quite simple. As a child develops from infancy to adulthood, there are changes in motivation, personality, and behavior that need to occur. One of these changes is a gradual growth toward independence and autonomy. With that comes a work ethic and a gradual responsiveness to the needs of others and the community that surrounds and supports one's life. Children leave behind the dependencies and irresponsibility of infancy, childhood, and adolescence as they move closer to adult roles. However, children's emotional maturity may not match their chronological age or grade level. The Ten Step Program offers parents a way to encourage and train maturity in their children. It fosters bonding, growth, and actualization of values and responsible freedom by training a child in follow-through, self-discipline, and accountability. This is why Step 1 may seem straightforward, but how it plays out may be complicated and troublesome for a while. The establishment of honesty, truth, and trust regarding schoolwork will be a measure of a child's growth toward maturity and adult freedoms and responsibilities.

Step 2: Set long-term and short-term goals.

Few parents (and fewer teachers) ever ask children to set concrete goals for academic achievement in school. This is unfortunate since underachievers seldom direct their behavior to specific goals in the classroom. Their goals are at best ill defined and vague, which means they avoid accountability for them-selves. At best, they become crisis oriented, responding with last-ditch efforts to just get by. The objective of this step is to establish the goals a child says he wants to achieve in school.

These decidedly are not the goals you want him to achieve. You must make it clear that the grades he states are what he truly wants for himself, what would make him proud of him-self. They are his goals, not yours. Initially, your child may not believe you mean that, but with consistency in applying this program, the vast majority of underachievers will begin to assert the values they have absorbed into their own conscience, a conscience they have absorbed over the years from being a child in your family. Underachievement is not a problem in values. Your child has already absorbed the right values from living in your family. Rather, underachievement is a problem a child has in realizing that success values are alive inside of him, and what he lacks is only the will to actualize them in his daily life.

The simplest way to approach this step is to have your child write down his classes on a sheet of paper. Beside each class, he notes the grades he would like to see on his report card at the end of a grading period. These are the long-term goals. Short-term goals are those grades he wants to make on individ-ual tests, quizzes, and projects that teachers assign him during the course of the grading period.

Parents should make sure that grades are specific, such as making a B in English or making an 85 on a specific test or project. The objective to "just pass," for example, is too vague, since "just pass" can be anything from the lowest D to the highest A. By making goals specific, you and your child will know when he has surpassed his goal, and you will know when he has failed to reach his goal. There is no equivocation on this. By asking your child for defined goals, you are taking the first steps to helping your child become more goal directed in his behavior.

Setting proper, concrete goals may make your child nervous, initially, and he may resist and complain. Resistance to goal setting almost always indicates a child is aware that by setting specific goals whose attainment can be measured, he has taken a small step on the larger road to accountability and responsibility. Do not be put off or become angry with your child's resistance to even this small step. A child's resistance to this process simply means you are hitting the right buttons, and you should proceed with confidence, kindness, and firmness in this matter.

Usually, at the beginning of the school year, most underachievers will indicate fairly high grades, such as all As and Bs. When this step is begun at the end of a bad grading period, most underachievers will indicate lower goals, such as Ds. Whatever grades he indicates he wants, accept them as his current standards and do not inquire too deeply at this point for his motivation for setting his standards. If you believe he has set his grades too high, such as wanting all 100s, you will be able to work with him as the school year progresses so that his grades are not so impossibly perfectionistic. If he sets his standards too low, which is more likely in the beginning of this program, your initial acceptance of his goals will set the stage for him to raise his own standards later.

There are many reasons why most underachievers set their grades too low. Almost always, the low goals they set initially are an artifact of what they think you really want from them, and they do not want to give in to you. Sometimes, they literally do not believe they can do well in school due to discouragement, self-esteem problems, and to the type of underachiever they are. The Ten Step Program will eventually tease out the underlying motivations and self-esteem problems that lead them to set artificially low standards. In my experience, the vast majority of underachievers begin to raise their own standards as you apply this program consistently. It is as though their initial reactions to goal setting were a kind of test of your commitment to be positive and accepting of their current limitations and discouragement. It has been my experience over the years that students will raise their standards more accurately to reflect their potential when they believe you honestly want them to live by their own conscience in this matter of grades in school.

Step 3: Explore how goals will be achieved.

The purpose of this step is to get as much detailed information as possible about your child's current academic behavior and course requirements. In this step, parents should ask, "How will you make these grades and get what you want?" Parents should ask about specific study habits and time spent on subjects after school. The aim is to get as full a picture as possible about what a child understands is required of him and how he goes about working. Questions about general study skills can also be asked as well.

This step may not be completed in one sitting, and the most worrisome classes may be the focus of attention. The requirements of a class or a specific project may change during a grading period so that this step may be repeated periodically throughout the school year. By asking these questions about requirements, parents focus their child on the details of school-work. By picking up details, it will be easier for a child to form plans for attacking his long-term goals on a daily basis.

What you as a parent will likely find in asking your child for this information are vague and inaccurate accounts of both study habits and requirements for success in his classes. Rarely are underachievers good observers of their own behavior, attitudes, and feelings in regard to academic achievement. To counter vagueness and poor self-observation, do not allow vague answers to stand without focusing on specific details. The purpose of this is to find gaps in your child's awareness of his own behavior and knowledge of scholastic demands. For example, if you ask him how much time he needs to study for an upcoming test, he may reply vaguely, "It depends." You should ask, "It depends on what?" "It depends" gives you no information about his intended behavior. What you are after is a specific goal and amount of time he believes he needs to spend studying to reach that goal. If he remains vague in his responses, make a note of these areas as follow-up points during the course of the grading period. Taking notes will allow you to slow down your own reactions and focus on getting a clear understanding of what your child knows and does not know about class requirements and his own study skills.

If your child's answers about his past behavior in school remain vague, focus on recent behavior, such as the time spent at home on various assignments earlier in the week. Good questions that lead to useful information include the time your child gets home, what were the sequence of his activities leading up to doing homework or studying, about how much time he actually spent on his subjects, when he took breaks, what time he quit, how much time he spent on other activities (such as playing on the computer, talking on the phone, watching television), and what time he went to bed. You can go through an entire week that way, and in doing this you and your child will get a clearer picture of the details of his evenings during the school week and how he prepared for his classes.

Your attitude should be nonconfrontational and nonjudgmental at this point. The whole inquiry should be done in the spirit of gaining baseline information both you and your child can use to prepare for changes he may need to make later. You should give no recommendations or advice and should certainly make no speculations as to his feelings and motives as this data gathering continues.

You are likely to encounter resistance from your child during this step. Underachievers correctly intuit that the more specific information they give, the more accountable they are for themselves. Since they are usually motivated to avoid feeling responsible for themselves, they are likely to complain about "all these questions" you are asking. An attitude of helpful neutrality is good to maintain, even if your child becomes testy and resentful. The resistance and hostility to this step covers the anxiety and discomfort your child is likely feeling on the inside. Maintenance of the Totally Positive Parent approach will teach your child that he can trust you to remain patient and kind, yet firm, just as you promised during Step 1.

Your child's emotional responses to your questions may also help you identify his type of underachievement pattern. For example, the Con Artist may become openly disdainful or try to smooth talk his way out of reporting to you. He may even try to make you feel guilty. The Socialite will find you boring, sigh, and roll his eyes heavenward soon after you begin this step. The Procrastinator will want to put off your talk or will begin to whine and complain that you expect more from him than he can give, and he may even become petulant and silent as you proceed. The Shy Type will get embarrassed or feel criticized. The Hidden Perfectionist may begin to fret and feel overwhelmed or just try to tell you what he thinks you want to hear so that things sound better than they are. The Martyr will begin to feel depressed and punished by your questions. These reactions reflect the kind of emotions that characterize your child's response to schoolwork and are involved in his continued underachievement in school.

When negative reactions in children do emerge from following these steps, parents often mistakenly feel they have done something wrong. No matter how I may have warned them that negative reactions are likely at various points during the Ten Step Program, they are surprised and sometimes shocked by their child's reactions. Some parents are even tempted to stop what they are doing and give in to their child's temper altogether, saying something like this: "Well, when he decides to do it, he will." Ironically, underachievers make dozens of decisions on a daily basis to arrange failure for themselves, but they refuse to recognize that they make those decisions. Until they see their decisions clearly and make conscious, concrete plans to change those decisions, underachievers seldom change their self-defeating patterns. The very program they rebel from is the one that will help them grow up. Underachievers are singularly ill equipped to be in charge of themselves, much less intimidate and boss their parents into leaving them alone. If parents cave in to their children's testiness and irritation, things almost always get worse, not better.

My message to parents is clear. If you are being rational, positive, and cooperative and your child is being negative, irrational, and rebellious, then your child has the problem, not you.

If you get negative reactions, remain positive. You should simply repeat the idea that you will help your child get what he says he wants out of his education. To be of help, you need information only your child knows. Sometimes it is helpful to simply repeat the question, "You do want to make better grades, don't you?" Underachievers almost always, even if reluctantly, answer yes.

Despite your best rational and positive behavior, some children may escalate their feelings until they start to get out of hand. If you feel that your conversation with your child has crossed a line and has become too negative, for whatever reason, you can call a break in your talk. Breaks should not last too long, only long enough for things to calm down, perhaps for fifteen or so minutes. Then you can go at it again. However, you cannot talk to an angry person. You can calmly tell your child to go to his room, and when he has cooled down enough to talk and listen, then you can resume your discussion.

Some children or teenagers feel that if they make a conversation with you frustrating enough, you will quit and leave them alone. You may have done exactly that in the past and have thus reinforced such thinking and behavior. Actually, you should do something to signal to your child that you have a good deal of time to invest in him and can spend it getting clear about school during this and the other steps to come.

One father I worked with developed a clever way of handling his easily irritated and impulsive teenage son. Whenever he set aside time to talk to his son about schoolwork, he wanted to indicate his commitment and devotion to helping his son do better in life. Once, he went out to the backyard patio, set a big cup of coffee on the patio table, and lay three rather large cigars on the same table. Then he called his son out to talk to him. He invited his son to sit in another chair, picked up one of the cigars, lit it, and puffed on it deliberately and slowly. He announced that he wanted to hear from his son all the reasons why he was not doing well in school and what he planned to do to raise his poor grades. He knew his son would want the conversation to be over quickly with as few words as possible. He used the cigars and the coffee to give a nonverbal indication of how long he was willing to spend listening to his son give an account of himself and that he had all day to devote to helping the boy improve his grades and his behavior.

In the first of these meetings, his son eyed the three cigars and the big cup of coffee and asked, "How long are we going to be here?" The father replied that he did not know how long it would take his son to deal with all his problems, but that he, his father, was in no hurry. He wanted to have a nice, quiet father and son talk about school. However long it took was fine with him. Throughout the conversations, whenever his son got too anxious or frustrated, his father would slow things down by relighting his cigar and taking a couple of puffs before responding. The ritual worked. Before long during that first meeting, his son realized that his father was serious and was not going to just go away, and that if he, the son, wanted more free time, he would have to become more cooperative and more disclosing. The quicker he gave information and thought through his problems, the sooner these "sessions," as he called them, would end.

I do not recommend that you take up drinking big cups of coffee or smoking cigars when you talk with your child or teenager about his education. However, if you choose your time for these talks wisely and signal that you have plenty of time to devote to these steps, then you will be more likely to get through them with good humor and a minimum of resistance. Perhaps you can develop little bonding rituals that signal you want and are willing to wait for a calm, significant conversation with your child about school. (Maybe you could have an herbal teatime?)

I do suggest that you make some notes on each of these meetings with your child. I believe you will find it useful to keep a journal about your talks, what information came from them, what your child told you, important insights you or your child may have had, and a note on the gaps in your child's knowledge. A good journal would also include the goals you are setting for you and your child, and how you believe things are going.

However, let me say that this step is not designed to teach your child study skills. The basics are all that is needed: how, when, where, and what to study in order to meet stated goals. Note taking, memorizing, listening skills, writing skills: all of these study-skill problems will emerge naturally later if they are even to become issues at all. What you are doing here as a parent is coming to understand what your child does and does not know about himself and what your child actually does to get what he wants. You are going to use this information to work with your child to identify ongoing problems your child should solve for himself. For example, suppose he says he believes that all the time he needs to spend studying each night is about an hour between 7:00 P.M. and 8:00 P.M. to make his As and Bs in school, but you notice that he does not begin work until 8:30 P.M. most nights and really only spends about twenty minutes on his work and his grades range from Fs to low Cs. Now, because you have done Step 3, you are in a position to help your child deal with this problem in his behavior; that is, deal with the fact that he is not doing what he said he would do to become successful. You are in a good position to use Socratic questions to increase his awareness of the difference between what he says he wants in life and what he actually does to sabotage getting what he says he wants. Now you have located a real problem to be solved.

Step 4: Select one problem and explore your child's perspective.

From one of the several problems or blocks you have found in your child's performance from Step 3, choose one problem that seems to you to be worthy enough to solve. One good way of selecting such a problem is to ask your child which of the problem areas that you have noted is the most important to change in some way for him to reach his goals. A good, worthy problem is one whose solution will help raise grades and at the same time will likely help you and your child reveal some of the underlying causes of his problems.

You may not always be able in the beginning of Step 4 to anticipate which of the problems your child presents you with will be the best one to reveal his inner workings. However, I have a rule of thumb. Any problem, once solved, that will raise grades, increase responsibility, and require self-discipline, is likely to be one of the problems that, by working on it, your child's inner life is revealed.

After you have chosen what you believe is a worthy problem to solve, the aim of Step 4 is to gain as complete an understanding of your child's perspective as possible on the problem that blocks him from getting the grades he says he wants. Get specific details with lots of concrete examples of how, when, where, and with whom the problem interferes with his grades, attention, or motivation, and who are those involved with his problem in either positive or negative ways. Get his behavior, attitudes, and feelings associated with the problem. Find out how long the problem has been going on in his life, when it started, and how often the problem happens to him. Leave no stone unturned. What you want is as complete an understanding as possible, as complete a picture in your mind as to what your child is experiencing when the problem under consideration emerges in his life.

I want you to take a moment to notice what is happening at this point. You are listening to your child tell you about his attitudes, feelings, motivations, and other aspects of his inner life! You have subtly shifted the balance of the conversation from blaming the world around him for his problems to the doorstep of personal responsibility: You are talking about what is inside of him.

Gaining the perspectives of Step 4 is not designed to make your child change his behavior, yet. It is to make your child feel heard and understood, so that he can have the experience of a positive, caring parent who takes the time to really listen to him before leaping to erroneous conclusions and providing more parent-imposed solutions to his problems. I cannot tell you how many times I have heard parents discussing their child's feelings, motivations, and private thoughts, and when I ask them how they know all those things are going on inside their youngster's mind, the parents usually point to the child's behavior. Behavior alone contains very important information, but it is never enough. The same behavior may be caused by quite different sets of motivations, intentions, and feelings in different individuals, and even at different times in the same individual.

In following Step 4, parents also give themselves a chance to gain a unique perspective on their child's inner life they would not otherwise have without following this step. This allows them to have one of the most powerful influences a parent can have on a child's development: deep empathy. Parents can actually come to feel what their child feels, even feel those feelings the child does not allow himself to experience directly. For example, when a child describes his problem as something others do to him, parents can usually easily feel the anger the child has, but the empathic parent can also feel what lies underneath the anger . . . the helplessness, shame, fear, and discouragement most underachievers hide by their resentments. Anger is easier to feel than helplessness. One can only feel the power of accurate empathy when one is calm and attentive to the other's inner world, and that empathy allows one to know another person, to stand inside his skin and know things his way. When a child feels that empathy from his parents, the bond in the family is strengthened, and the parents can use the wisdom of adulthood to guide them in helping their child through his problems.

Gaining your child's perspective and isolating his reasons for failure are the steps most often missing from the more directive approaches to influencing student motivation and success, such as reward and punishment systems, tutoring, study-skills training, and power tactics. Without gaining your child's point of view, approaches to help him will likely fail to win his deepest cooperation and commitment, which in the long run are necessary, even essential, to overcoming chronic underachievement and discouragement.

By pursuing a detailed understanding of your child's perspective and feelings about a significant problem, two things are usually revealed. One is that your child, like most discouraged children, is vague about himself and how he functions. The vagueness is crucial, for one of the ways children and adolescents remain locked into self-defeat is by failing to analyze their problems in specific and concrete enough ways to even know what to change. Your focus on the important details of experience and analysis of your child's perspective in this step begins the process of overcoming helplessness and discouragement by allowing your child access to enough information about himself to lay down plans for successful change in academic behavior and attitudes toward learning.

The second thing a detailed questioning usually reveals is a good excuse for failure. Excuses are reasons your child uses to justify or explain away failures and poor performance. At the heart of any excuse used by an underachiever is the insidious perception the student has of himself or others. Permanently overcoming discouragement and underachievement involves changing distortions in thinking and perception. For example, the student who says he has failed history because it is boring is likely operating on the mistaken belief that his feelings are the world's responsibility to solve for him, and that if something is boring, he should not be expected to do anything about that, much less work. It is the teacher's responsibility to make him excited enough to do his homework and learn. A child's feeling of responsibility for his own emotional states, such as boredom, needs to change. For the purposes of Step 4, it is important to gain the student's perspective without challenging these distortions and immature perceptions directly. Below is a transcript of one of my cases where we were working in Step 4.

PROFESSIONAL: How did you get such a lousy grade in English?

STUDENT: I don't know. I just didn't like it.

PROFESSIONAL: Didn't like it? What is it that you don't like about English?

STUDENT: Well, grammar and literature. It's boring.

PROFESSIONAL: Well, you know, I know what boring means to me, but I'm not sure what "boring" means to you. What is boredom like for you?

STUDENT: It's not interesting. I don't like it. I didn't want to do the homework.

PROFESSIONAL: Did you do the homework anyway?

STUDENT: No. Well, some of it. I guess I got zeros. I made good grades on my tests, though. Mostly Cs and Bs.

PROFESSIONAL: So, the zeros on homework led to your making an F in English the last six weeks?

STUDENT: Yeah, but it's so boring that I can't make myself concentrate. I want to do the work, but when I sit down to do it, suddenly, I'm daydreaming. Some days, I just can't make myself get started. I just put it off . . . then it's too late.

PROFESSIONAL: What do you do when you are bored?

STUDENT: I try to find something to do.

PROFESSIONAL: That's more interesting?

STUDENT: Yeah. I watch TV or call my friends, shoot baskets, maybe.

PROFESSIONAL: What else do you do when you are bored?

STUDENT: Well, I get sleepy. I can't concentrate.

PROFESSIONAL: So when you get bored with English, you don't do the homework, is that right?

STUDENT: Yeah.

PROFESSIONAL: And when you can't concentrate, you quit working on homework and try to find something more interesting to do?

TUDENT: Yeah, that's right.

Although more work needs to be done in understanding the student's perspective on negative feelings in general, this type of exchange is enough to establish several good excuses for failure. These are: 1) boredom; 2) lack of concentration; 3) not wanting to do the work; 4) daydreaming; and 5) procrastination. It would be important to notice that each of these excuses begins with his helplessness and inability to handle the feeling of boredom.

If you are alert during similar exchanges with your child, you may notice the helplessness implied by his excuses. It is as though another power had taken over your child and short-circuited the ability and willingness to cope with negative emotions and attitudes.

One helpful thing I could have done during the above exchange with the student would to have reflected back to him the underlying feelings or perceptions I was hearing from him. When he said, "I can't make myself concentrate . . . I just can't make myself get started," I could have asked, "How do you feel about being so helpless when you are bored?" I call such responses "reflective" because they mirror back to the individual what he is saying about himself without his necessarily being aware that he is saying it. The student in the above exchange was not conscious of his helplessness, but everything he said indicated he had no alternatives but to respond in the self-defeating ways he usually did in those circumstances.

Reflective responses are very important, nonthreatening ways to help a discouraged child understand himself better and to redefine the underachievement problem in ways that will allow a child to be more flexible and creative in his life and ultimately, to exert more self-control. Obviously, as long as this student continued to define himself as helpless, with lots of "I cants," then he would perceive himself as being unable to change and his responses would remain rigid, inflexible, and self-defeating. If on the other hand, he begins to see the boredom as his problem to solve and not someone else's problem, then he can begin to take steps to become competent in handling negative emotions and attitudes and enhance his life accordingly.

If you, as a parent, are actively listening to how your child is construing his experiences in school through excuses, then generating reflective responses will be easier than it may seem at first. However, even if you make no reflective responses during the course of this step, I advise you to write down the excuses your child makes. By writing them down, you ensure you will focus on these excuses, and you will serve notice to him that you will take what he says seriously.

Even though although mildly depressed individuals often complain of boredom, the focus of Step 4 is not to talk about depression or lecture a child on how if he did his work he would feel better. The sole function of this step is to isolate and elaborate the child's view of his excuses and reasons for failure and to provide rich enough detail on the student's personal experience so that the foundations for change are well laid for the near future in other steps.

Step 5: Link your child's problem to goal attainment or failure.

This may seem like an obvious step to most reasonable individuals. However, I have learned that underachievers often miss the obvious or ignore it at the most crucial times. In following the Ten Step Program, never assume that what is obvious to you is equally clear to others. Make the obvious very clear: make it shine under the bright shimmering light of your precisely focused intelligence and insight.

The aim of this step is to ensure your child understands the connections between his excuses or problem and his failures to achieve his own goals in school. The link between the problem and its natural and usual consequences in his life should be done bluntly, clearly, and without artifice to avoid any ambiguity about the message.

Remember, discouraged children hide their discouragement and anxieties about the future by severing the connection between today and tomorrow, between what they do today and the consequences tomorrow. They say they would like to avoid bad grades, and then take specific actions or nonactions today that hasten those very consequences without really being aware of what they are doing at the time. They perceive themselves and others around them in ways that allow them to remain unconscious of their decisions and actions that lead to self-defeat and failure.

A child with severe procrastination problems almost always sees himself as acting reasonably when he puts assignments off until later, even though almost every time he has done so in the past it has led directly to a failure of some kind. Each time he puts off work, he intends eventually to do it, although he rarely does on his own. Retrospectively, he can see the pattern of procrastination and underachievement. In the moment of actually procrastinating, however, he does not see the danger.

In this step, you are setting your child up to surrender his denial of self-defeating behavior through insight, planning, and decision. This is why you must first make the link between the problem and its consequences very obvious, and lead him through the linkage. By failing to see the link between today and tomorrow, underachievers avoid facing their own decisions to fail. By establishing clearly the linkage of today's excuse with tomorrow's outcome, a child's conscience is linked to his behavior. The child begins to see how he defeats what he himself values, which tends to build up an inner pressure within him to change. An example of this linking process is as follows.

PROFESSIONAL: It seems that almost every time you get bored with English, you do not do your homework.

STUDENT: Yeah, pretty much.

PROFESSIONAL: Yeah. That's really a tough thing, isn't it, because what happens if you don't solve that problem?

STUDENT: Uh, I don't know. I guess I won't turn in homework again.

PROFESSIONAL: Yes. And then what will happen?

STUDENT: Well, I guess I'll make a really bad grade.

PROFESSIONAL: Seems like that's so. So what do you say about that, since you want to make a B in English?

STUDENT: I don't know. I guess I'll make a bad grade?

PROFESSIONAL: Do you want to do that?

STUDENT: No, but what can I do? I've tried everything.

PROFESSIONAL: That's a good question.

Notice that in the transcript how I took pains to make the connection between the excuse and failure clear to the student. The student was able to articulate the connection, after which he expressed plainly a sense of helplessness and discouragement in being unable to solve the problem.

Expressions of helplessness and discouragement are often heard from students once they are made to see the connection between preparation and grades in a specific instance. The danger here is that as his parent, you may try to console or reassure your child that the problem is easy to solve, and offer the obvious solutions, such as study skills or "just do your work" advice. As stated before, most underachievers are quite capable of coming up with appropriate solutions to their problems and it is a dependency-inviting reaction for you to supply solutions for him. More importantly, the process of change is never an easy one. Discouraged children fight against their fears of the future by fighting achievement battles. Simple reassurances are misguided and are apt to make discouraged children more discouraged when they inevitably fail to carry out the supposedly "simple" solutions offered by others. The proper attitude you, the parent, can take is a nondefensive, nonattacking, "laid back" emotional approach. In this way, your child is more likely to respond with a nondefensive reaction as well.

Chapter 14

Getting to the Heart

What you have established in the previous chapter is setting the stage for change to begin. Now, you want to try to get to the heart of your child's problems in the next five steps (Steps 6 through 10).

The next five steps, in fact, the whole Ten Step Program, is designed to lead you and your child into the heart of his choices to fail. It is there at the level of your children's choices where you and your children together will discover the previously hidden causes of underachievement. When these causes of failure are revealed, then feelings of empowerment can replace helplessness, understanding can replace ignorance and anger, and change can replace stagnation and failure.

The next steps offer a way of leading underachievers to a crossroads where they are practically forced by circumstances they have helped create to acknowledge responsibility for their own problems. Leading underachievers to the crossroads is done by focusing on the symptoms of underachievement in a special way that will eventually lead the underachievers back on themselves as the cause of their problems. This special way is basically to engage the underachievers in setting up their own plans to solve problems and overcome blocks to getting the kind of grades they say they want for themselves. The overall plan of the Ten Step Program is to constantly and concretely connect the underachievers' behavior and attitudes today with tomorrow's goals.

By following these ten steps, underachievers are led to a greater awareness of the difference between what they say they want and what they actually do on a daily basis to sabotage their goals. They are led by their own plans to see how inconsistent they are, how they stop work, what feelings and attitudes are involved in their underachievement, and to believe they are responsible for changing themselves. Often they are even led to see that they often want conflicting things, and they will have to finally make up their minds as to what they stand for in life. When underachievers say they want good grades, but would rather play than work, then they have been brought to a moment of decision, a crossroads in their development.

Once children are at the crossroads of a decision and the decision is analyzed in accordance to the processes to be explained below, then most underachievers will begin to grow more responsible and more successful. They will also disclose more information about themselves, which helps parents know their children better. If children or adolescents do not grow more adultlike and more stable in their self-discipline, then parents may have to take over some of their children's behavior and restrict freedoms in accordance with how immature they are acting. For example, if a sixteen-year-old adolescent underachiever now understands how self-defeating he is and knows he is making consistent decisions to choose short-term pleasures over the achievement of long-term goals he also wants, then do you let such a child have access to a potentially deadly apparatus, such as a car? Parents should restrict the use of a car by tying it not to grades alone, but to responsible decisions. When children want to act more like an adult in one area of life, i.e., drive a car, then they must act more like adults in another area of life, i.e., handle school more responsibly. In other words, the parents sometimes have to admit to themselves that their children really are not mature enough to handle some responsibilities if they are not mature enough to handle others. They must relate to their children by their true maturity level and not just what they think is normal for their age. In following the next steps, these kinds of issues come to the forefront and parents can make decisions about freedoms and responsibilities based on the emerging information about the true maturity revealed in their children's responses to the steps below.

Step 6: Help your child make concrete plans to solve achievement problems.

The major purpose of this step is to place the child in the position of being unable to avoid responsibility for his actions. The problem has been identified and an agreement has been reached about the importance of doing something about it. The child now has to give solutions to the problem. The cycle of intellectual dependency, where the child looks to you for answers and then rebels *must* be broken. *DO NOT SUPPLY SOLUTIONS OF YOUR OWN:* YOU WILL ONLY CREATE MORE DEPENDENCY IF YOU DO.

Parents should assume the attitude of innocence and help-fulness. Parents are not asking for a preconceived list of an-swers, but for the child to generate potential solutions from his own head. Once the child is engaged in the process of thinking of good solutions, good questions from parents can guide his thinking. Such good questions may often involve coming up with all the potential snags in the proposed solutions, and then asking the child how he would handle these.

Resistance from children is the rule during this step. There are usually lots of "I don't knows," or even "Don't ask me." Do not get angry. If a child is too resistive, then a parent may need professional assistance. However, many children simply need to understand that the parent is both patient and serious about the child doing his own thinking. I have recommended that parents of an "I don't know" child send the child to his room or the kitchen table for an indeterminate length of time to think alone.

When the child has come up with a few ideas he can discuss with the parents, then the child and his parents can try again. Often, children will ask how long they have to sit at the table. Parents should say something like, "Oh, I don't know. However long it takes you to come up with some ideas on your own. But whenever you are ready, let me know. If you need the time, we can spend the whole weekend on it. But whenever you have thought about some solutions you would like and we have discussed it, then you can have free time again." Once the children understand that they could spend the whole week-end at the kitchen table doing nothing else but thinking about the problem, they find they have some thoughts in their heads after all.

Once a solution has been offered, even if it is vague, parents should go with it and discuss it in detail. A good plan is one that is specific, concrete, and one that can be monitored or observed in the child's behavior. A good plan is also one that if actually followed would very likely lead to success. All the potential hitches and snags should be discussed and subplans made to account for them.

Often, arriving at a good plan of action requires the patience of Job for worried parents. This is often a tedious step with children making it hard through passive and at times vociferous resistance. Actually, it is important to know that when parents evoke their children's resistance to getting better, they are doing their children a great favor. Nothing of any importance is ever accomplished with most underachievers without evoking their resistance because underneath the resistance lurks the subterranean fears and shadowy motivations that the child does not want to confront, but which also cause him to fail. Patience, time, and compassion are needed for this step. Remember Socrates, Columbo, and above all, Mr. Rogers. Parents may need all the good imagery they can muster within themselves to stay calm and committed through this step.

As a training tool, I play a game of creating solutions to problems while making the teaching nature of the game obvious. Lack of knowledge of problem-solving brainstorming may not actually be the case. However, I have found that it is better to assume ignorance first than to assume willful resistance or passive avoidance of a task. By playing a training game, I am allowing a child to save face if he is simply opposing me, and change himself. The following is an example of this approach with a thirteen-year-old male underachiever of excellent intellectual potential.

PROFESSIONAL: I can see you have difficulty thinking of possible solutions to this problem. Have you ever done anything like this before?

STUDENT: I don't think so.

PROFESSIONAL: Well, let me teach you how to create possible solutions to problems. First, let's play a teaching game. Let's make an easy one for learning purposes. How could you get from the couch to this chair over here?

STUDENT: Well, I could just walk over there and sit down.

PROFESSIONAL: That's right. How else could you do it?

STUDENT: What do you mean?

PROFESSIONAL: For purposes of this game, think of other ways you could get to that chair. Creative ways. Not necessarily practical ones.

STUDENT: I could crawl. I could roll on the floor.

PROFESSIONAL: That's right. And you could think of lots of interesting ways. You could get a boat to China, catch a plane to India. Hitchhike across Europe, fly to America, catch a cab to my office and go upstairs. Cut a hole in the ceiling over my chair, and then lower yourself by rope into the seat. Those are some ways. All of them would get you to the chair. Some are just more efficient than others, but all are good and correct ways to solve the problem. After creating a bunch of solutions, you'd just choose the one you wanted. Do you get the idea of creating solutions?

STUDENT: Yeah, I think so.

PROFESSIONAL: Good, then let's come up with some possibilities for doing your homework and making those good grades in English. You can create several, yet not commit to any one of them.

Naturally, if a child continues to shut down, then parents will have to deal with this child's dependencies and emotional problems. Parents may have to seek help from a professional to help them. Very often, however, discouraged children can be coaxed to present effective solutions to the problem in question, especially when the parents are patient, kind, and persistent. Often, discouraged children will create solutions that parents believe will not work. Your best bet is to go with the proposed solution and wait for a failure to occur. If you have done your job well enough, then your child will not be able to avoid feeling responsible for his behavior, which sets the stage for real changes in his motivation for success. In one of my own cases, I was working with a fifteen-year-old young man with a "memory" problem. In Steps 1 through 5, we identified several problems with remembering to bring work home, remembering assignments, and even remembering to turn in work when he had actually done it. In going through his daily routines, he recounted another recurring problem in getting home on time. From my interviews with his parents and with him, I learned that he was supposed to be home by 5:30 P.M. to start his work. Inevitably, he would forget most of the time and arrive at home late, sometimes as late as 6:30 P.M. He and his parents fought battles over coming home on time. They had tried grounding and taking away privileges, even tried getting off work early to get him home. Sometimes, he would get home on time, and at other times he would forget.

The problem was that when he got home late, he would start studying late. He would get home, usually about the time his parents arrived home from work, about 6:00 P.M. Then he would have to rest from his play and eat supper about 7:00 P.M. to 7:30 P.M. He would let his food digest for about half an hour. Then he would start studying about 8:00 P.M. or so. After several breaks for phone calls and other sundry things, 9:30 would come around and he would be too tired to study or do homework anymore. He would promise himself to get up early to finish his work or study for tests. Inevitably, he would arise late, rush to school, and not have time to finish studying or doing homework. Sometimes he would forget homework at home in his rush to get ready. Therefore, he would make poor grades on tests and zeros on homework. His grades, thereby, would suffer.

The young man and I agreed that getting home on time would be a good problem to solve. If he got home at 5:30 P.M., then he could start studying earlier and finish his homework and study longer for his tests. If he did these things, he expressed confidence his grades would come up. Getting home on time, then, was the first step in a sequence of events that would lead him to get better grades. Now he needed a plan as to how he was going to solve that problem. Below is a partial transcript of a conversation I had with him during this planning.

STUDENT: I get busy and involved with my friends and I lose track of time. I don't get home until late, so it's after supper before I get started studying most of the time.

PROFESSIONAL: If you were going to get your work done, then what would be the best time for you to be home?

STUDENT: Five-thirty.

PROFESSIONAL: Where are you normally after you get home from school?

STUDENT: I usually get home around four, get a snack, and then go down the street to play ball with some of my friends. I don't get very far away from home.

PROFESSIONAL: You set five-thirty as a goal. If you don't make it, what happens?

STUDENT: Well, I wind up not doing some of my work. I get zeros.

PROFESSIONAL: In other words, by not getting home on time, you actually get things started the wrong way. It leads to zeros and bad grades.

STUDENT: Yeah.

PROFESSIONAL: How can you remember to come home?

STUDENT: I don't know.

PROFESSIONAL: What time would you have to leave your friend's house to make it home by five-thirty?

STUDENT: Five-twenty.

PROFESSIONAL: How could you make sure you leave your friend's house on time?

STUDENT: Well, I'll just tell myself how important it is to remember to get home on time.

PROFESSIONAL: Hmm, haven't you done that in the past?

STUDENT: What?

PROFESSIONAL: Reminded yourself how important it was for you to get home on time.

STUDENT: Yeah.

PROFESSIONAL: It didn't work did it?

STUDENT: (Shakes head, "No.")

PROFESSIONAL: So, what are you going to do since you cannot rely on that strategy?

STUDENT: Well, I could think really, really hard to remember and tell myself how really, really important it was to get home. I could write myself little notes and leave them places as reminders.

PROFESSIONAL: Sure, you could do that. But, what if you do all of that, and you are playing basketball with your friends, how will you make sure that at 5:20 P.M. you will remember to come home? Your notes won't be there, or if they are, you could forget to look at them.

STUDENT: I could get my friends to remind me. (Comment: notice how he is transferring dependency to his friends. I could have chosen to talk about making himself dependent on his friends, but I chose to stick with the Ten Step approach completely for this young man.)

PROFESSIONAL: Do you think that will work?

STUDENT: Well, it could.

PROFESSIONAL: What happens if they forget to remind you? Do you really think they can be your memory for you?

STUDENT: No, I guess not.

PROFESSIONAL: Are you stuck? With your memory problems, do you have any other ideas?

STUDENT: No, not really. I'll just have to rely on my memory.

PROFESSIONAL: You know, that just has not worked too well in the past. What are you going to do tomorrow and the next day and the next after that?

STUDENT: (Silence.)

PROFESSIONAL: You do want to make better grades, right?

STUDENT: I just can't think of anything.

PROFESSIONAL: You know, I can see you are at the end of your road here. You are stuck. You might need some time alone to think. I'll tell you what. I'll just leave my office for about fifteen minutes or so. If you haven't thought of some ideas by then, I'm sure I can let you have even more time if you need it. (I get up to leave, and he stops me at the door.)

STUDENT: Wait, I've got an idea. I could set the alarm on my watch. It would go off at 5:20 P.M., and when it went off, that would tell me it was time to come home. Then I could come home by 5:30 P.M.

(Comment: It's amazing how much creative thinking a child can do when he knows you are serious about his using his own brains, not yours, for answers. However, I have often said that you, as parents, should leave no stone unturned in gaining a concrete plan to solve a real problem in your child's life. If you think we have covered all bases, please read on.)

PROFESSIONAL: That sounds like a good plan to me. How do you feel about it?

STUDENT: I think that will work.

PROFESSIONAL: That's really good, then. Oh, just one more question. When will you set the alarm on your watch?

STUDENT: As soon as I get home. (Comment: I saw this as a typical maneuver to escape responsibility and accountability. So I asked the next question.)

PROFESSIONAL: But, what about your memory problem? I mean, what if you forget to set your watch when you get home?

STUDENT: I'll write myself a note right now about how important it is to set my watch. I'll think, it's really really important.

(COMMENT: As you can see, he is relying on the same old failed strategies of the past. Actually, this moment had the quality of game playing. He was beginning to sense that old self-discouraging strategies were not effective, and he was being weaned from them. I also sensed that he was looking for an opening. He was going to see if I would allow him to do something that even he was dimly aware was a loophole in his usual way of functioning. In other words, he was testing me with this. Am I going to hold him accountable? You bet.)

PROFESSIONAL: Well, you know, your memory has failed you in the past. What happens if you forget to look at your note?

STUDENT: Yeah. I suppose I should set it now, huh?

PROFESSIONAL: Do you have a problem with that?

STUDENT: No. (He sets the watch alarm.)

The same process of getting a detailed and practical plan can be done for any excuse or problem your child may generate. In the above example, the student was placed in the position of having a plan worked out in detail to take care of one of his chronic problems in school. The plan he worked out was reasonable and was actually better than the ideas I was having in my own head when I was listening to him.

Once you have defined a concrete plan of action, you are ready for the next critical step in this program, Step 7. This next step sets the hook. Once Step 6 is done, you have hooked your child into his own conscience by bringing him to the crossroads of freedom in his life.

Step 7: Redefine success and failure as following his own plans—analyze the decisions he must make to succeed or fail.

The purpose of this step is of great importance to the process of being successful and building character in children. The purpose is to redefine success as actually following through with the plan the child has created and failure is redefined as not following the plan. Grades are not important here. Following the plan is. In other words, all attention is now focused away from the goals of getting grades and the new goals become actually carrying out the various steps of the plan itself. Success is following the plan. Failure is not following the plan. This must be made clear to the child and the child needs to articulate this redefinition.

It is also very critical that the parents help their child analyze the decisions he will need to make if he is to follow his plan. Any good plan has decision points built into it, points in time where a child must actually decide to sit down and work. Controlling attention, handling boredom, coming home on time, sitting down to work at a desk, writing assignments down: these are all decisions children make and underachievers must be aware, too, if they are actually to change their lives in school, build new habits, and create new destinies for themselves. Therefore, parents must isolate these critical decision points and ask their child if he decides to actually follow his plan at that point, what kind of decision he will make. The answer: the decision to be successful. If he decides to procrastinate or not follow his plan, he needs to articulate the future consequences, and if he decides to follow it, he needs to articulate the future consequences of that decision as well.

This careful review of decisions and consequences is necessary because it helps children become aware that there are no simple decisions for a particular moment, that a decision now has consequences and the consequences are the inevitable results of the decision. This makes children aware that both achievement and underachievement result from decisions they make, and they are ultimately in control of their decisions. If they are unhappy with the results, then they can change the decisions they make, and by going over the decisions, they will know precisely what decisions to keep making or what new decision to make next time.

Most underachievers almost always hate to see that they make decisions at all. They prefer to see failure as outside their control. If an analysis of decisions is thorough enough, then even the most resistive underachievers will begin to feel more personally responsible for what happens to them, and by the way, more worried. When underachievers become more worried and anxious about themselves, rather than angry and rebellious or passive and dependent, then they have the emotional basis for developing new motivations in life.

Below, I will continue with the transcript I used in Step 6. This transcript will illustrate how I brought the young man to his crossroads. You will recall we left him setting the alarm on his watch as a plan to get home on time so he could study.

PROFESSIONAL: Have you set your watch?
STUDENT: Yeah.

PROFESSIONAL: I've gotten kind of confused. What is your plan?

STUDENT: Well, I come home from school, and I have free time. Then my watch alarm goes off. Then I come home by 5:30. Then I start studying.

PROFESSIONAL: Hm. Is that all that's happening here?

STUDENT: What do you mean?

PROFESSIONAL: What I mean is this. You'll be out playing with your friends, right? Say you're playing basketball, okay?

STUDENT: Okay.

PROFESSIONAL: You're having a lot of fun. You don't really want to leave. Suddenly, your alarm goes off. Right?

STUDENT: Uh-huh.

PROFESSIONAL: What happens after you turn off the alarm?

STUDENT: I go home.

PROFESSIONAL: Well, going home is not automatic, is it? I mean, you're not a robot, are you? What will have to go on inside you for you to really leave and come home?

STUDENT: Well, I'll have to think, "It's time to come home." Then I'll go home.

PROFESSIONAL: Right. There you'll have to make a decision. You'll have to make a decision to come home.

STUDENT: I see, I think. I'll make a decision to come home.

PROFESSIONAL: And if you do decide to come home, what kind of decision are you making here?

STUDENT: A good one.

PROFESSIONAL: (Laughs) Well, you might be right. But what would make that a "good" decision?

STUDENT: Well, a decision to go home and study. Then I could make better grades.

PROFESSIONAL: Well, look, even before the good grades come.

You have this plan, right? Then if you decide to come home when the alarm goes off, aren't you following your plan?

STUDENT: Oh, yeah. I see. I'll be doing what I said.

PROFESSIONAL: Right. You will be successful in following your own plan. You are being successful right now because you have already started following your own plan when you set your alarm.

STUDENT: Oh, I see. Right.

PROFESSIONAL: Now when your alarm goes off and you make a decision to go home and you actually go home, aren't you being successful at that point?

STUDENT: Yeah, it's also a way to get better grades.

PROFESSIONAL: But what if the alarm goes off, you turn it off, and you make a decision to stay and play with your friends some more? What kind of decision is that?

STUDENT: A bad one.

PROFESSIONAL: But how is it bad?

STUDENT: It's a decision to not get home on time and to not really study like I said.

PROFESSIONAL: Then what?

STUDENT: That's what I've done in the past. I screw up that way.

PROFESSIONAL: You mess up in school and make poor grades. So what are you really deciding when you make a decision to come home?

STUDENT: I'm deciding to make better grades. Or, to give myself a chance.

PROFESSIONAL: And if you decide to stay with your friends?

STUDENT: (Sighs audibly) To mess up.

This part of the transcript illustrates a redefinition of the problem from "forgetting" to get home on time to making decisions to succeed or fail. In the beginning work with this student, he was helpless because he could not do anything with his "memory" problem. As a result of following the Ten Step Program up to this point, we have been successful in coming up with a pretty good plan for taking care of a memory problem and redefining the emotional situation from one of helplessness to one of personal power. He is empowered by the fact that he now recognizes that he has a plan that will work and that he is the one who will decide to either make it work or make it fail by his decisions and his behavior.

In one of my seminars on discouraged children, I was using this transcript to train parents to follow these procedures when a very astute parent asked me what happens if he still did not come home and still used the excuse that he forgot? Then he added, "Suppose he loses his watch or forgets to wear it?"

When you get to this point in the Ten Step Program, you are actually unhooking a child from his favorite excuses. Remember, in earlier chapters of this book, I discussed the function of excuses was to remove a child from anxiety and worry about his own behavior. Excuses function to keep a child from feeling responsible for himself. Even if this particular child had come back with either option—he forgot to come home or he forgot his watch—the original excuse would have been rendered ineffective. Once he recognizes the connection between an excuse and a failure, and he has a concrete plan to remedy that problem, and once he has recognized he will make decisions to succeed or fail in carrying out the plan, and then he recognizes how carrying out the plan will enable him to get what he says he wants (better grades), then it becomes very difficult to not recognize all those connections, and still feel no anxiety or guilt in failing to carry out the plan. So far, all seven steps have edged the child closer to responsibility. When one knows one will decide to succeed or fail, then excuses do not even make sense.

In truth, once you have completed this step, the child may actually follow through and solve this one little problem. However, he may choose to substitute a new problem or excuse in place of the old one. That is, he may "forget" his watch. Although this type of what I call "excuse substitution" does happen, it does not mean the Ten Step Program is dead. Rather, the child now has another problem to solve, and you keep using the Ten Step Program to solve it.

Underachievement is much like becoming lost in a great living maze. There are many blind alleys that lead nowhere and therefore, many ways to lose oneself in the maze. There are also many ways to find one's way out. Many parents think there should be only one way out and once you have found it, then underachievers need never be lost in the maze again. This is not so. Yet, when a child finds his way out of the maze once, he never needs to become lost *that way* again. Of course, he may get lost another way. Eventually, after many mistakes and many setbacks, one learns the ways of the maze and one hardly ever becomes lost again. The Ten Step Program offers a way to help an underachiever learn enough about himself and how he defeats himself to master the maze that is himself. Every time your child becomes lost in his own maze of underachievement, you simply have another opportunity to help him find his own way out once again. As a loving parent, you should welcome every chance for your child to learn the hidden ways of his routes to failure. This way, you help him build a solid foundation of self-knowledge that eventually allows him to become more successful and more in control of himself.

As you will discover in the steps below, following these steps weans a child from his excuses and exposes the real inner problems. Step 8 is designed to further hook a child into responsibility by gently exposing more decisions and possible conflicts. When you complete Step 7, you will not be through, yet.

Step 8: Initiate introspection—explore conflicts and feelings about following his plans.

The purpose of this step is to initiate your child's introspection. All decisions to break old habits create doubts and misgivings in all underachievers. The purpose of this step is to help a child learn to talk about those conflicts and emotions.

Parents should help their child acknowledge both good and bad feelings and the good and bad consequences that occur when they follow through with their plans. There are sacrifices and gains in any life decision. Underachievers see that they will sacrifice having fun or other pleasures for the pain of working at something they dislike and may not want to do. By helping a child articulate the price he will choose to pay following his plan, he can experience his parents' full understanding of what he goes through emotionally. Underachievers find self-discipline painful. The good feelings that come from success and self-discipline are subtle, and they will not experience them for a while.

Steps 7 and 8 are powerful tools to help children understand that they actually make decisions whether they want to or not.

It is difficult to maintain old excuses and irresponsibility when children have explored success and failure as decisions and behavior over which they have total control. Some unsuspecting parents may find at this point that it is the very experience of autonomous control and self-authority that many underachievers most fear and avoid. This step allows parents to gain access to the central conflict in most underachievers: the desire to remain dependent and resentful versus becoming more independent and responsible. This step also allows parents to help their children redefine their feelings from negative ones about doing work to positive ones.

During this step, you want to establish feeling positive as a goal, as well. The goal of having positive feelings connected with following through on a plan is an important component of sustained achievement. In the long run, it is difficult for underachievers to do well, partially because they usually connect negative feelings about school and themselves to studying or doing homework. Learning is negative. For the young man in the example in Step 7, and for all underachievers, the ability to even acknowledge the possibility of feeling good about follow-through on their plans may be difficult. They usually have attitudes and thoughts that lead them to feel negative emotions about schoolwork, parents, and learning. Ideally, discouraged children need to identify these negative attitudes and feelings, take responsibility for them, and change them or substitute positive attitudes and feelings for them so that studying, learning, and school become much more positive.

The way this is done is simply to ask your child how he would like to feel about following through on his plan. Especially in the beginning of this approach, your child probably will not know what you are talking about. It is a foreign notion to most kids (and to some of their parents) that an individual can actually decide to have good feelings about work. Your child will not likely be much different from most other under-achievers in this regard. In fact, do not be too surprised to find in the beginning that your child does not want to change his negative feelings about learning and doing schoolwork. How-ever, if you are persistent in asking if he would like to feel good about following through on his plans, you will begin to wean him from negative feelings. After all, most of us adults have had the experience of having to do stupid school assign-ments in the past, and I can remember not wanting to feel any differently about those "stupid" assignments (and I still feel they were stupid, too!). However, your child may and can choose to feel good about getting even stupid assignments done, and he can certainly feel good about reaching his own goals. Feeling good about finishing tasks, following his plans, and reaching his own goals are what you should be pointing to with this step.

Further, most underachievers have lots of ideas and feelings swirling around in their minds when they have to do school-work. Many children, underachievers and achievers alike, often think of many things they would rather do than sit home and do schoolwork. They often feel a conflict. Underachievers more often decide to play rather than work. Part of this step is to gently expose some of those conflicts about doing work. Once exposed, children will feel even more understood and helped.

However, do not expect miracles. Independent children who can be their own bosses will make decisions to work, whereas dependent children who cannot be their own bosses will inevi-tably make decisions to avoid work. By engaging in this step with your child, you will make dependence and independence an issue you can address as time goes on.

Below, I will continue with the transcript I used in the previous step. This transcript illustrates how you can weave this step in with Step 7.

As you may recall from Step 7, we left "Student" sighing and saying that if he chose to stay with his friends when the alarm on his watch went off, then he was choosing to fail at his own plan. Step 8 was initiated at this point in the conversation with him.

PROFESSIONAL: Sounds like coming home from being with your friends does not make you happy?

STUDENT: No, that's all right. I'll go home.

PROFESSIONAL: Yeah, I know. You do want to go home, but I was just thinking from your reaction just now that you might not be happy to go home. I mean, I could understand that feeling.

STUDENT: I guess I'd rather stay and not have homework.

PROFESSIONAL: I can understand that. (It is important, I believe, to let kids know that we adults, too, would rather not have work to do at times. His feelings are understandable.) But you are going to come home anyway, right?

STUDENT: Yeah, I guess so.

PROFESSIONAL: Couldn't you want to stay and be with your friends and still go home at 5:20 to do your work?

STUDENT: Yeah.

PROFESSIONAL: That is your plan, isn't it?

STUDENT: (Nods, "Yes.")

PROFESSIONAL: Well, how would you like to feel about following your plan and coming home when the alarm goes off?

STUDENT: Huh?

PROFESSIONAL: You know, when your alarm goes off and you actually go home to study—how would you like to feel about that?

STUDENT: Well, I don't know. How am I supposed to feel? (Comment: This is a real question for this young man and for many underachievers. Basically, this young man is a Hidden Perfectionist type of underachiever, and this type of underachiever often has trouble knowing how they actually do feel about things. In truth, he is always concerned over what he is *supposed* to think, feel, do, and say, and how he *should* act. He is not usually concerned with how he actually does think, feel, and act. The overconcern with the "shoulds" keeps him locked in a constricted, passive rebellion. The rule of thumb here is this. When a child asks how he should feel, ask him how he actually does feel, if he is satisfied with feeling that way, and if he would like to feel differently.)

PROFESSIONAL: Supposed to feel? How do you actually feel when you go home to study?

STUDENT: Bad. Kind of mad. I can think of a lot of other things I'd rather do.

PROFESSIONAL: Sure you can. But, do you want bad grades?

STUDENT: No.

PROFESSIONAL: So are you sure you would rather do other things than go home to study?

STUDENT: Well, right then, I'd rather not go home. But I

guess for the long run, I'd rather go home and finish my work.

PROFESSIONAL: So just right then when the alarm goes off, say, you'd really want to stay to be with your friends for right then, but the next day in class you would rather have your work done. Is that what you mean?

STUDENT: Yeah, that's it exactly. I guess I put things off and enjoy myself for a little while, but I screw myself up later.

PROFESSIONAL: Well, how would you like to feel about going home to study when your alarm goes off tomorrow.

STUDENT: I guess I should feel good.

PROFESSIONAL: Why should you feel good about doing what you want?

STUDENT: Because I'm choosing to get better grades.

PROFESSIONAL: Do you like getting what you want out of life?

STUDENT: Yeah. But I don't always want to do homework. Well, uh, I guess I do want to do it, don't I? So, I guess I'd want to feel good about going home.

PROFESSIONAL: Well, you could have mixed feelings. You could regret not playing more with your friends, but you could also feel good about going home and taking care of your learning, too.

STUDENT: I guess I could do that.

PROFESSIONAL: Well, since you have decided today to actually go home when your alarm goes off, you could notice how you actually feel and then we would talk about that next week when you come back.

STUDENT: You mean whether I feel good or bad about going home to work?

PROFESSIONAL: Right. We could talk about your real feelings. Maybe, then, we could work on connecting good feelings with going home on time. What do you think about doing that?

STUDENT: Yeah. So I'll figure out how I feel about going home, and I'll try to feel good about it, too.

PROFESSIONAL: Does that sound like a good idea to you?

STUDENT: Yeah, it does. I'll try it.

By initiating an introspection in Step 8, this student identified troublesome emotional conflicts as well as potential resolutions to them. One conflict was his desire to do well in school versus his desire to have fun with his friends. I wanted both desires to be accepted by him as legitimate, worthy desires. Too often, parents give their children the message that play is not legitimate or worthy, only doing schoolwork is. At least, kids often come to feel that way. Further, I wanted him to experience the conflict between his desire for good grades and desire for play as things he wanted for himself, and by making a rational decision, he could actually have both. I wanted to attack his latent perception, which many underachievers have, that work is parents' and teachers' idea and play is the kids' idea. Finally, I wanted him to experience the conflict as something within himself and that the responsibility for resolving that conflict was something he would decide and, thus inescapably, his responsibility.

Another aim of the introspective focus was to redefine the usual problem of getting home on time. In the past, the student secretly resented the feeling of having to go home. He responded to his parents' demand (in truth, the demand of his own conscience) with procrastination, excuse making, and avoidance of feelings of responsibility for his decisions.

In this Step 8, anger was uprooted by his acceptance of a redefinition of the situation on two levels. The first level, discussed above, was that going home on time was now his idea so that he could have a chance to get what he said he wanted in school: better grades. The second level of redefinition was to introduce the emotional goals into the process of decision making. Because of Step 8, he is introduced to the idea, which he found both confusing and intriguing, that he could find a way to feel good about coming home because he would be doing something to get the good grades he said he wanted for himself. If he could find a way to make himself feel more positive about following his own plan, then anger about coming home is irrelevant.

Of course, changing one's feelings is sometimes quite difficult. So, I wanted to make sure I let him know that any feeling about coming home was fine with me. I only wanted him to notice what they actually were. Sometimes, especially in any introspective moment with a child or adolescent, a new agenda for future discussion may arise. Connecting positive feelings with follow-through on work and plans for success is definitely something I wished to establish as a future point of discussion with this young man. For the time being, letting him know that I was comfortable with any feeling he may actually have or wish to have about following his plan was my way of telling him that I accept him the way he is right now without any conditions. I did not want him to believe he had to have other emotions than he actually experienced just to gain my approval. Too often, discouraged children believe they have to have only feelings and thoughts acceptable to others, or they will be rejected. Frankly, if a child wants to go to school, bring work home, do his work and do it well, make good grades, and hate every minute of it, be my guest! My experience teaches me that whenever you give children the right to hang on to their negative emotions, the irrationality of hating what they choose to do to secure goals becomes so obvious they will often give up their negative feelings on their own accord. However, I always offer my aid in the alchemy of emotional transformation.

Step 8 may be one of the more complicated steps in this program. It is difficult to know how far to take a child in exploring his conflicts and emotions. Your best rule, as a parent, is to explore only those feelings bound up with the concrete plan and the task under discussion in the moment. In terms of feelings, stay in the here and now.

In truth, however, most alienated, discouraged children and adolescents are not at first going to launch into an introspective look at their behavior, thoughts, and feelings with you, anyway. They have to trust themselves with their feelings and their self-disclosures, and they have to trust you, that you will not use their feelings against them. My advice is that you should go forward with trying to understand your child's thoughts, feelings, and conflicts only as far as he can go. In other words, do not push very much during this step. Make yourself more like a mirror. Reflect back to your child what he is saying to you. Let him lead you. Eventually, after following these steps over and over again patiently, while you remain positive parents, your child will likely gain more trust in himself and in you when he talks to you.

You gain closure on Step 8 after you have discussed introspective material enough to indicate you understand your child's feelings and conflicts, and that you accept him. This solidifies planning. When you have done this, you are ready for Step 9.

Step 9: Cement commitments to follow through on plans.

This is probably one of the easier steps to accomplish in the whole Ten Step Program. Yet, like all the others, it is an important step that you do not want to leave out.

At this point in your progress, you have identified patterns of study behavior, some of the demands on your child in school, set goals, obtained problems and conflicts in meeting those goals, made concrete and specific plans to overcome any problems in meeting those goals, anticipated any snags, and developed subgoals and subplans for handling potential snags successfully, and you have tied your child down to specific decisions and consequences of either following through or failing to follow through with his plans to get what he says he wants. At each step you are gaining more and more information on your child's functioning and gaining increased commitments. Hopefully, you are remaining positive, even if your child is not. You have just finished with the final touches in Step 8 in exploring your child's personal feelings, thoughts, and conflicts about follow-through and exploring the potential of connecting positive feelings to follow-through. Now that you have finished all of this, in your best imitation of a combination of Mr. Rogers and Columbo, you ask what may at first sound like the silliest, most simpleminded question. "Now that you have this plan all worked out, what are you going to do, really?"

In my experience, it is always safe for a parent to assume that all the while your child has been talking to you and committing to each step of this program, he has been having another, more secret, stream of thoughts inside him, perhaps just below the level of his awareness. All throughout he has been saying to himself something like this, "I'm really not going to do all this stuff. I'll just go through the motions for a few days until all of this blows over, and then I'll go back to normal." This step is designed to make him state one more final commitment to follow through on what he said he would do to get what he said he wanted out of his life.

Whenever I ask a child or adolescent this question, "Now that you have this plan, what are you going to do, really?" I almost always get a surprised look. It is as though I have guessed some of his inner thoughts. So far, I have never had a child or adolescent give a negative response to that question. After going through all of the previous steps, then to say, "No, I'm not going to do anything we've talked about," would be tantamount to admitting that his real goal is to sabotage his own best interests in life.

However, I have had some kids respond with doubt and anxiety about their ability to follow their plan consistently enough to change. Doubt is usually expressed by the child saying something like, "Well, I'll try." If your child expresses anxiety about his ability to follow through, accept his doubts and acknowledge them in a positive and supportive manner. Tell him that if he is not able to follow his plan and do better, then you will certainly listen to that message. Tell him that it may be that he is too dependent on you or his mom and he cannot be his own boss in these matters. If so, you will certainly be glad to step in and help him out as needed. Assure him, for now, that his effort is all you are asking for.

Doubt and anxiety are fairly rare early in the Ten Step Program. Usually, most kids respond that they will, of course, do what they have said they will do. You should be eager to find out if they do follow-through.

Step 10: Detailed follow-up and a sequence analysis of his specific decisions to succeed or fail.

The purpose of this step is for you to take the time to follow up on what your child actually did with his plan. Did he actually choose to be successful in doing what he said, or did he choose to fail with it? Did he bring his books home from school like he said, or did he "forget" them again. In the case of the individual whose transcript I am presenting here, did the student actually come home on time when the alarm went off on his watch or not?

There are only two possibilities with this step. Either your child followed through or he did not. Whether he did or did not follow through, you need to ask him questions that will detail how he either succeeded or failed. What you are looking to gain is what I call a "sequence analysis."

All social behavior and especially all planned behavior occur in a sequence of events. These events include "inner" events and "outer" events. Inner events include such things as wishes, thoughts, instructions to oneself, judgments, memory, emotions, and values. Some of these inner events can be observed, such as when a child shows his emotions and attitudes, but often, the child must report what goes on inside of him. Part of a "sequence analysis" is to get your child to tell you about these inner events, or what goes on inside of him as he goes about succeeding or failing to follow through with his plan.

"Outer" events are those actions a camera would reveal if it were used as a recorder of events. The idea is that your child reports to you how things happened, as though a camera were recording them. These events are most often elicited by asking questions such as what happened, what happened next, and then what happened, starting from the beginning to the end.

A sequence analysis could look like this. Johnny comes home from school and places his books down on the dining room table. He gets something to eat and then goes out to play. He comes home around 5:00 P.M. and looks at his books on the table. He then goes to the living room to watch television. He eats supper. He walks through the dining room to use the telephone in the den. He talks on the phone off and on until 9:00 P.M. He falls asleep around 9:30 P.M. He wakes up and dashes off to school. He did not turn in his homework because "I forgot to do it," he later says. This is the outer part of a sequence analysis.

An inner sequence includes the outer, but focuses on inner events. For example, Johnny comes home from school and places his books down on the dining room table. He remembers he had an English assignment due the next day. After playing, he comes back home around 5:00 P.M. and looks at his book on the table. He thinks, "I'll do English later." Yet, he never thinks about his English assignment again.

Both the inner and outer events are critical to understanding what happened so that Johnny did not get his English assignment done and for unhooking the excuse that he "forgot" to do it. Under this analysis, Johnny would have shown clearly that he did remember to do his English. When he remembered to do it, however, he chose to go do something else, which, at the moment, meant he chose to take a chance on failure once more. Thus, through a complete sequence analysis, Johnny can come to understand that he makes decisions to fail and that different decisions were, are, and will continue to be possible.

A good sequence analysis is obtained when you can piece together a complete picture in your own mind as to how your child performed in carrying out or failing to carry out his plan. In other words, if your child follows through with his plan, you want a sequential picture of how he did it. If he failed, you want a sequential picture of how he failed.

The purpose of a sequential analysis is to bring a discouraged child into responsible accountability, finish unhooking excuses, reveal information about your child's emotions and perceptions you may not otherwise get, reveal weaknesses, encourage self-monitoring, and reveal more of the underlying problems. Obviously, a sequence analysis is not always a simple thing to obtain. An example of a sequence analysis will be helpful in clarifying how its purposes are fulfilled. Before I give an example, however, I need to digress a moment to clarify the heart of this step.

The heart of Step 10 is to increase self-monitoring abilities in your child. Self-monitoring is a crucial maturational skill that, unless something goes awry in a child's psychological development, increases with age. Self-monitoring is an awareness process that allows us to know what we are experiencing in terms of thoughts, feelings, moods, and perceptions, and also to know the causes and sources of those inner states. Self-monitoring allows you to know, for example, that you are mad at your child because of something in you, or because of something your child is doing to create anger in you. Self-monitoring also allows you to be aware of alternative actions and feelings you could have at any given moment with your child. Because self-monitoring enables one to be aware of alternative actions and beliefs, I consider self-monitoring to be a precursor skill, one that precedes the possibility of choice. Without awareness of alternatives that self-monitoring makes possible, choice may be impossible. Thus, self-monitoring skills allow freedom of choice to exist on the personal level.

Self-monitoring helps prevent emotional contagion. Emotional contagion occurs when an individual actually feels swept away by the emotions of other people. If you have ever seen laughter ripple through an audience in a theater or seen anger fire up a previously passive mob into violence, then you have an idea of what emotional contagion is on a group scale. If your child has ever thrown a roaring temper tantrum at the counter in a crowded grocery store because he could not have the candy he wanted, and you became enraged by his anger, then you know what emotional contagion is on the personal level. When self-monitoring is a mature skill, the individual can know from whence his feelings come and remain free to participate in the emotions of others, or remain aloof and respond differently. Through self-monitoring, one has some immunity against emotional contagion and some freedom of choice about one's feelings.

Through self-monitoring we come to know our typical patterns of behavior. If that particular pattern of behavior is a problem, we, by being aware of it, are more likely to change than if we remain unaware of our own behavior patterns. An individual skilled in self-monitoring is able to see how his behavior affects others in their responses to him, and he can see how his responses to others and to the task demands of his life affect him over time. What I do today will have consequences tomorrow. Through consequences, we learn about ourselves, we learn from mistakes and from successes. But we can only learn if we monitor ourselves and know from whence we have come.

I once worked with a bright high school student who was a Socialite underachiever. She could monitor the behavior of others quite well, but not her own. After undergoing intensive work in the Ten Step Program, she became increasingly aware of how she discouraged and defeated herself in school. She eventually assumed responsibility for her life and her decisions.

At the end of her first semester in college, which was successful, she came in to see me to relate an incident that for her signaled a fundamental change in her approach to achievement. She told me that she had been in the library studying for a difficult exam the next day. She said that her mind had soon begun to drift, and she caught herself daydreaming about her new boyfriend. However, when she caught herself daydreaming, she admonished herself. "I knew that this is just what I had done in high school to defeat myself. I'd think about things other than studying," she told me. "I decided not to let that happen anymore, so I went right back to studying. I was really proud of myself." Pride in oneself and freedom of choice often go hand in hand. By becoming aware of what she was doing, through the skill of monitoring herself, she was able to exercise real freedom and take power over her behavior.

This story is a good example of the power self-monitoring makes possible in one's life. She caught herself daydreaming and by connecting this daydreaming with a pattern of daydreaming in high school, by which she had defeated her potential, she was able to exert her freedom of choice and chose a different path for her life. As a matter of fact, she was actually able to learn to control her attention span so well that she allotted herself a time to daydream and a time to concentrate on achievement. By monitoring herself, she attained more of a balance in her life.

I will discuss the other purpose of Step 10 as the presentation of cases continues. For now, let us look at an example of how success is handled in Step 10.

In the transcript I have been presenting, the student came up with a plan that would get him home on time. All eight previous steps were completed, and now, he had to follow through or fail.

PROFESSIONAL: I'm interested to know how getting home on time went for you last week and this week.

STUDENT: It went well. (Comment: This is typical of most underachievers. They are afraid or reluctant to reveal details openly and forthrightly about themselves.)

PROFESSIONAL: Tell me more about it. (Comment: I recommend that you, parents, ask for more information with such phrases as I have used here. Simply and politely request more information.)

STUDENT: Well, I got home on time, like I was supposed to, every day.

PROFESSIONAL: On time? You mean you got home by 5:30 P.M. every day?

STUDENT: Yes.

PROFESSIONAL: How did you do that?

STUDENT: Really, it was easy. When my alarm on my watch went off, I remembered I needed to get home.

PROFESSIONAL: How do you feel about being successful like that?

STUDENT: Pretty good. You know, it wasn't that hard, really. It turned out to be no big deal. I was playing basketball and when my alarm sounded, I just came on home. A couple of times, there wasn't much to do, so I just came home early.

PROFESSIONAL: When your alarm went off and you were playing with your friends, what were your thoughts?

STUDENT: It's time to go home. A couple of times I wanted to stay, but I knew what I needed to do. (Comment: Some of you who are reading this text may be thinking that having to come to my office and confront me about his behavior may have been an incentive to follow through. You may be quite right. Accountability to another individual is always central to developing intrinsic motivation. Accountability to oneself and one's conscience is an act of autonomy that comes later in an individual's development, when the individual realizes he cannot escape his own conscience.)

PROFESSIONAL: Now, remember last week, I asked you to notice any feelings you had about following your plan, whether you had positive or negative ones. How about your feelings?

STUDENT: Toward the end of the week I felt pretty good about myself. I feel pretty neutral about it right now. It does not feel like that big of a deal. It's something I can do easily.

PROFESSIONAL: Well, there was a time you struggled with this.

STUDENT: Yeah, I know. I guess I've changed a little.

PROFESSIONAL: Can you see any snags coming up that would prevent you from getting home on time in the future? Any problems?

STUDENT: No, not really.

PROFESSIONAL: You can continue to get home on time?

STUDENT: No problem.

By analyzing success, I am sending a signal that success is as important as failure. One can learn from both. The child may also learn that following a plan and starting a new habit is not the earth shaking burden it may seem at first, especially when the individual takes responsibility for following through and executing his plan. After this type of analysis of a success, then you are ready to keep repeating these steps until change occurs.

A sequence analysis of failure is often more tricky than with success, however. The tricky part is to remain calm, curious, and positive while your child may be sullen, angry, and uncooperative. You, the parents, should remember that every failure is an opportunity to learn more about the puzzling maze of underachievement and self-discouragement and to do the hard work of finding a way out of that maze for you and your child.

The most productive attitude you can take is that failure can teach important lessons about success if attention is focused on learning, not on punishment, guilt, or defending self-esteem. A good sequence analysis often sets up the next problem to solve by helping define how the failure really occurred. Further, it often totally unhooks your child from his excuse for failure. Moreover, a good sequence analysis conducted with compassion and understanding can make your child feel rewarded for his introspection and cooperation with you. Finally, a good sequence analysis reveals the decision point that led to failure, allows you to discuss old decisions and what decisions your child could make next time and, thus, reinforces a sense of responsibility and feeling of control.

However, you may not always be able to remain a calm combination of Columbo and Mr. Rogers, especially if your child stubbornly refuses to answer your questions. One thing I've noticed that helps in dealing with an underachiever is a fundamental belief in the power of persistence. Persistence pays off. Perseverance and patience are Biblical virtues you can cultivate to become both a better parent and a better person. Let us focus, now, on a case of a sequence analysis of a failure.

This student, Student 2, was a seventeen-year-old young woman who had chronic problems with grades and motivation in school. In the current grading period of this transcript, she was failing two subjects. We focused on science. As part of our work, I asked her to bring me her science notebook so that I could get a better understanding of what she did not understand in science that was supposedly causing her to make poor grades. She claimed that the material in her notebook was too confusing for her to understand. As her teacher used printed handouts more than the textbook for examinations, I felt if I saw the handouts in her notebook, I would be better able to comprehend her difficulties and help her with a reasonable plan to overcome her lack of understanding. She actually agreed wholeheartedly with me, and she made a good, concrete plan to bring me the notebook the following week. Because she had the nearly ubiquitous underachiever memory problems, the plan also included how she was going to remember to bring me her notebook the next week's session. That plan included leaving notes to herself and having her father remind her the morning of the day of our next session. Without going into further details about her plan, it was a complete plan evolved out of the first nine steps of the Ten Step Program, and it was one she could follow and agreed to follow.

When the next session rolled around, however, she did not have her science notebook. "I forgot it at school," she said.

It was obvious that to her "I forgot" was a sufficient and reasonable explanation that needed no further elaboration. Intuitively, I felt she wanted me simply to accept the excuse as a face-saving device to spare her the embarrassment of explaining what happened to her carefully constructed plan to remember to bring her notebook. I am sure most parents in my situation would not have probed the sequence of events that lead to her forgetting her assignment. However, helping underachievers change their lives means not doing the socially polite thing. You, as the parent, must also choose the moral and realistic point of view and not the socially polite one if you want your child to change. Polite manners are merely the clothes we wear when we hunt for the truth relentlessly. Manners temper the fierceness of our search, but they are a poor substitute for it.

PROFESSIONAL: That's too bad. Now, I'm not able to really see what you don't understand. I'm not able to help you very much like you had wanted last week. How do you feel about not having your notebook?

STUDENT 2: I'll bring it next time.

PROFESSIONAL: You know, I was just now wondering something. I remember your careful plans to remember your notebook. How did you forget your science notebook?

STUDENT 2: I don't know what you mean. I just forgot it, that's all.

PROFESSIONAL: Well, what I'm trying to understand is how that occurred. Just how your day went. For instance, did your father remind you this morning about getting the notebook here as you requested of him?

STUDENT 2: Yes, he told me.

PROFESSIONAL: So, at that point you did remember to get your book?

STUDENT: Sure.

PROFESSIONAL: Well, did you think about it anytime during the day in school?

STUDENT: Yeah, a couple of times. Look, what's the big deal here. Everyone forgets things sometimes. I just forgot, that's all. I'll get it next time.

(Comment: This student hates to know the details of her life. She is beginning to feel uncomfortable with this line of questioning for it is bringing her to realize that "forgetting" is not all that happened to her. She does not want to know what happened and is feeling defensive about my inquiries. I imagine that most parents at this point would discontinue any further questions because of their child's anger. Do not be afraid of an adolescent's anger. Anger is often a way of making others go away. by inducing guilt and anxiety. As I did, you will simply continue to ask reasonable questions in a firm but nice way. Furthermore, appeals to how "everyone" forgets is another way of avoiding personal responsibility. After all, if everyone else does something, then it must mean that I am less personally accountable for my individual actions, right? Wrong. The whole point of this Ten Step Program is to bring an individual to an accounting of their personal conscience so that individual moral choice is even possible, and that the development of individual motivation and creativity are possible as well. If you expect more individuality from your child than a creature of the herd, then when your child gets angry, you know you are hitting the right buttons, so take heart and continue.)

PROFESSIONAL: I'm happy that you will bring the notebook next time. And you are right. Everyone forgets things from time to time. I know I do. But knowing that everyone else sometimes forgets important things says nothing at all about how you, personally, forgot your notebook. All I'm trying to understand is how this forgetting happened to you. Right now, I care most about you, not everyone else on the planet. Remember, your original idea was to go by your locker after sixth period to get your notebook, right?

STUDENT 2: (Calmer, now.) Yes, that's right. I'd planned that.

PROFESSIONAL: Now, let your mind go back to sixth period today. At anytime during sixth period or right afterward, say at the bell, did the thought cross your mind that you would get your science notebook?

STUDENT 2: Well, twice, I think. Once during class and once

right after the bell rang and I was on my way to my locker, like always.

PROFESSIONAL: So you were on your way to your locker and you thought about needing to get your notebook?

STUDENT 2: Yes.

PROFESSIONAL: That's helpful. So what happened next?

STUDENT 2: Well, I went to my locker.

PROFESSIONAL: (I expected her to go on, but she remained silent. After a pregnant pause, I continued.) What happened when you got to your locker?

STUDENT 2: Several of my friends were there. We were talking and stuff. They were leaving, so I grabbed one of my notebooks and caught up to them. I didn't know at the time I had grabbed the wrong one until I was getting ready to come here, tonight. That's when I realized I had the wrong one.

(Comment: Now we are getting to the real story behind the excuse of forgetting. There is always another story to be told that is different from the one underachievers usually present to gloss over their choices. This girl was more concerned about her friends than with following through with her own plan. Her desire to succeed in school and an important plan to help was lost at the locker in favor of juvenile herd instincts. Adolescents almost always believe peer approval and acceptance is more important than becoming a functional adult. Yet, the peer group often disperses after high school, and many kids who have not been properly initiated into full adult behavior often find themselves lost and may remain lost, as many grandparents can testify. One purpose of the Ten Step Program is to initiate immature kids into adulthood by unhooking excuses and having kids focus on decisions and responsibility. Unhooking the excuse is what comes next in the transcript.)

PROFESSIONAL: Oh, whew! Man, am I relieved to hear what you've just said. Thank goodness!

STUDENT 2: (Truly perplexed.) What are you talking about?

PROFESSIONAL: Well, for a moment I thought you might have a serious learning disability or memory problem or something. But thank goodness you've just cleared that up and I'm greatly relieved not to have to refer you to a neurologist.

STUDENT 2: Huh?

PROFESSIONAL: Look, like you just said, you did not really forget your science book after all. On several occasions, even when you were at your locker, you actually did remember to get your science book and bring it here to my office. Your memory worked fine. You really did not forget to bring me your science book. Aren't you relieved?

STUDENT 2: (Feeling more anxious now.) No, I don't have it. I forgot.

PROFESSIONAL: No, you did not forget. You just said that at least four times today you actually remembered you were going to get your notebook. In fact, you even remembered to go to your locker after sixth period to get it. You even remembered it well enough to open your locker and to actually reach in to get your notebook. No, your memory worked quite well, after all.

STUDENT 2: (More petulant.) I don't know what the big deal is, I'll bring it next time.

PROFESSIONAL: Right. But now we know more about the real problem.

Student 2: What do you mean?

PROFESSIONAL: Hmm, I was wondering. What color is your science notebook?

STUDENT 2: They are all the same color, white.

PROFESSIONAL: All of them are white? The same shade of white?

STUDENT 2: Yes, all white. Why?

PROFESSIONAL: You keep them all in your locker?

STUDENT 2: Yes. They're lined up, all side by side.

PROFESSIONAL: Side by side.

STUDENT 2: Yes.

PROFESSIONAL: Now, let me see if I got things straight. You remembered to get your notebook, so you actually went to your locker after school to get it, right so far?

STUDENT 2: Yes.

PROFESSIONAL: Now, there are several of your friends at your locker about to leave, and you wanted to go with them . . .

STUDENT 2: Yes.

PROFESSIONAL: So you opened your locker . . .

STUDENT 2: Uh-huh.

PROFESSIONAL: And you reached in to get your science notebook, which was the exact same color as all your other notebooks, then you grabbed one of the notebooks, shut your locker, and left with your friends, the wrong notebook in tow.

Student 2: Yeah.

Professional: You know, isn't there something wrong here?

Student 2: I don't know what you mean.

Professional: Well, did the thought occur to you that maybe, since all your notebooks were the same color, that maybe you should check to see if you have the right notebook?

Student 2: I thought I had it.

Professional: I know you thought you did. But looking back, when you reached quickly for the notebook to grab one to then catch up with your friends, you really had a decision to make at that point, didn't you?

Student 2: I don't know. What decision?

Professional: Well, to check and see if you had the right notebook, your science notebook. Since they all looked exactly alike, would it not have been reasonable for you to wonder if you had grabbed the correct one or not? Did the thought occur to you to check to make sure you had the correct book?

Student 2: Yeah, maybe I should have checked, but I was in a hurry.

Professional: That's what I understood. But look, when the thought occurred to you to check to see if you had the right notebook, what did you do next?

Student 2: I just grabbed one. I didn't think anymore about it. I grabbed one and caught up with my friends.

Professional: So when you had the thought "I should check my notebook," you did something else instead.

Student 2: (Nods, "Yes.")

Professional: You did not check to make sure. That's when you had a decision to make. When the thought occurred to you to check your notebook, you could have made a decision to check, but instead, you chose to ignore your thought, take a chance on failure here, and instead, choose to be with your friends.

STUDENT 2: Yes, I suppose it happened that way. I could have done things differently, I guess.

PROFESSIONAL: Has that happened to you before in your life? Where you make a choice to be with friends rather than take care of school commitments and, therefore, wind up failing something as a consequence?

STUDENT 2: Sounds like I've done that before, huh?

PROFESSIONAL: So what are you going to do next week when you go to your locker?

STUDENT 2: I'm going to check.

When this young lady left my office, she was terribly angry with me. She told her mother that I had no right to question her the way I did and that she was never going back to see me again. She also called me a few choice names, the mother told me later. Fortunately, this mother was not intimidated by her teenager's righteous indignation over not being allowed to remain irresponsible. The mother simply said that her daughter would continue to go to the sessions and that, eventually, when she was older and more mature, she would understand that I had just done her a favor.

In follow-up sessions with this student, she never again used the excuse that she "forgot" something. She brought her notebook in the next session, and she became calmer and more self-disclosing in future sessions.

However, that session did reveal that she could have made

a decision to make herself more successful and that she defeated herself when she did not listen to her own success-related thoughts. By not listening and following her own success-oriented thoughts, she followed self-defeating social-oriented thoughts and increased her feelings of inadequacy.

Further, I felt that this session showed that her anger at me was really a cover-up for her sense of inadequacy. She felt humiliated and angry at me for focusing on the details of her behavior and decisions. Her embarrassment came not from my searching for the truth, but from her own values by which she secretly judged herself to be inadequate. This session laid the groundwork for focusing on her values, feelings, and choices in future sessions, thus supporting greater awareness of her true self and helping her establish a stronger identity that eventually helped her grow beyond chronic feelings of inadequacy with a concomitant push for compensatory social approval. For her, this session was a first step toward accepting more complete responsibility for her own life.

A word about comfort in working with adolescents in this Ten Step Program. Many parents with whom I've consulted over the years have a seriously mistaken belief that it is their job to make their children happy, successful, and comfortable. Anytime their children are anxious, uncomfortable, unhappy, or unsuccessful, these parents take action to make their kids happy, comfortable, or successful. It is as though these parents are afraid their children will suffer in life, or they fear their children's disapproval and rejection. As a result, these parents often overprotect their children on the one hand by rescuing them from problems and giving in to their children's demands. On the other hand, when frustrated and angry over their children's misbehavior, laziness, and shallow values, these same parents overreact with punishment that only makes matters worse.

One of the reasons most underachievers continue to defeat themselves is that they remain oriented to pleasures of the moment at the neglect of long-term goals and self-interest. They wind up getting long-term pain and close doors to their future. They can maintain their painful lifestyle only by focusing their energies on short-term pleasures and ignoring their own values for achievement. They discourage themselves by not only ignoring important ideals and values within themselves, but they also discourage themselves through the resultant aimlessness and purposelessness of their lives, through the loss of talent and potential, and through the failure to develop adequate competencies for today's world. By not developing competency in an area of life as important to their future as school, discouraged children are failing in the development of an identity that will support the demands of adulthood. As a result of this failure at the level of identity development, these children and adolescents threaten to become Peter Pans, the lost boys and girls of never-never land who fail to grow up. They become imposters of adults. They look and talk like adults. They certainly age like adults. They can do things adults do, like make money, drink alcohol and play adult games, have sex and make children. But emotionally and at the level of values, they are not adults, and it is a mistake to treat them so. At the core, these individuals live lives of desperation and uncertainty, which they try to hide by relying on excuses in place of effective living.

The purpose of following the Ten Step Program outlined in

this book is to reverse short-term comfort for long-term pain, by gently but insistently focusing on responsibility and on decisions that lead to failure. In this way, the excuses and denial of underachievers are stripped away to reveal the true child underneath. Without their excuses and denials, the emotional pain and suffering of most underachievers will be starkly revealed. In other words, as the excuses go, the discomfort level rises, the anxiety increases, and sometimes, raw emotions spill out. This is good. Your role, as a parent, is not always to make your child comfortable. Your role, sometimes, is to do things that lead your child to feel uncomfortable with their own behavior.

I want underachievers to become uncomfortable with their excuse-making, self-defeating living. Once they are uncomfortable enough with what they are doing to themselves and others, most underachievers will be more willing to listen and work harder in their lives. Especially if parents are firm, supportive, and positive with their children, then their children will be more willing to expose their pain and find the guidance they need to change for the better. Before a child can reveal his pain, he must believe in his parents' care.

There is a trap parents typically fall into, however. Perhaps you have thought that once you have completed Steps 1 through 9 in this program, your child is bound to be successful in following his plan. After all, he has set his goals, you have been positive and inquisitively helpful, he has set a plan he can follow and has committed himself to follow, and he knows that if he does not follow it he invites failure and if he follows it he invites success, which he says he wants. Yet, even after all of this has been done and done well, you will likely be greatly disappointed and overly frustrated if you expect your child to actually follow through with his plan. Expectation of follow-through is a trap to snare you into negative feelings and discouragement as a parent. Remember, your child has not developed the virtues of seasoned achievers, and he has intentions and motivations that have led him to sabotage himself in the past. Therefore, lack of follow-through is one of his major problems in life and it will not likely be cured just because a rational, self-enhancing and life-enhancing plan has been established. I always like to withhold my expectations and adopt a wait-and-see attitude. I want to see what the underachiever actually chooses to do. I know if Steps 1 through 9 have been done well enough, in the one small area of his life the plans are for, the individual has been brought to the crossroads from which there is no returning. He is at the crossroads of conscious choice, and in his choice he will reveal the work that remains to be done.

In effect, by so far following the nine previous steps, you have given your child only four basic options.

Option One: He can make the decision to follow through with his plan and start getting better grades and taking more responsibility. This is a fairly popular choice with many underachievers. It is difficult to openly choose a path of failure when one knows one is choosing failure.

Option Two: He can decide not to do the work and become emotionally responsible for his motives to make bad grades. This is the least popular option and few underachievers actually choose it. Those that do are often so discouraged that they do not believe in themselves and are so hopeless that they may suffer from a paralyzing depression, which needs to be treated. Other kids who choose this option may do so out of defiance and rebellion and deeply felt disappointment in adults and the adult world. Such children, whether depressed or lost in rebellion, are in such psychological difficulty that extensive psychotherapy and family therapy are probably required to correct these problems. At least the choice of Option Two makes the inner realities of the child quite clear.

Option Three: He decides he does not wish to follow his original plan, but he gets his work done anyway. I, or any other reasonable person, have no quarrel with this option. I want only to know what is the plan he has chosen and does he wish to continue with it? In school and in life, plans can change. But to go from having one plan to having no plan is itself a plan, a plan for potential failure.

Option Four: He can substitute a new excuse or problem for the original one. Actually, this is the most popular response in the initial run-through of the Ten Step Program. Now, he may offer a new excuse to replace the older, obsolete one, or he may reveal an emotional or motivational problem that lay hidden under the obsolete excuse. Both of these outcomes are good events.

What's Next

From now on, until the problem is solved, simply repeat the previous ten steps. Unhook excuses, denials, and undo blocks to achievement that surface through use of the Ten Step Program.

The point of recycling the steps of this program is that in so doing, parents establish a relationship with their children that protect their autonomy, while at the same time, parents are able to confront irresponsibility and hold their children accountable for decisions and behavior. By going through these steps over and over again, parents will gradually wean their children from their excuses and their denials, which is valuable in uncovering their real intentions and motivations that block them from success. Even more important for the long-run maturity and success of underachieving children, parents will be weaning them from the process of excuse making itself. The idea is to lead kids into an awareness that they are making excuses and to become uncomfortable with themselves when they make them.

The spirit of the Ten Step Program is to increase communication between parents and their children so that, hopefully, parents will have a better understanding of the roots of their children's problems. As children's reliance on excuses wane and their anxiety goes up accordingly, parents who continue to follow the principles and steps of the Ten Step Program are able to maintain emotional distance and to more effectively and accurately listen to their children. Emotional distance and accurate understanding helps children feel autonomous, which is critically important, especially in the teenage years.

Adolescents need to believe that parents will not make them into the parents' clones. By continuing to cycle through the Ten Step Program while following the principles of positive parenting, parents are sending a message that they will not force control of their children unless absolutely necessary and not without giving them plenty of chances to overcome failures on their own. When underachievers start doing better under these conditions, they overcome discouragement and take more ownership of their work and responsibilities. Doing well in school, in other words, becomes the children's idea, not only the parents' goals for them. Most people do better when their labor is voluntary, not forced. The same is true for children.

As a result of recycling the Ten Step Program, children may reveal emotions, beliefs, intentions, attitudes, and motives that prevent or block them from being successful. This is a likely outcome if children are weaned from many excuses over time. Once exposed, parents can begin to deal with the emotional and motivational realities of their children rather than the false masks of denial and excuses offered in place of reality. Parents will have gone below the surface farce of their children's lives and will have entered into the deeper layers where the mother lode of motivation exists. This is where parents can help heal the wounds that fester within their children. When parents hit an emotional barrier to achievement, they should be glad. No matter how upset their children become when the barriers are reached, no matter what emotions, attitudes, or motives are revealed there, no matter how disturbing these wounds appear to be at first, parents should actually rejoice in discovering the sources of pain, for they have hit true pay dirt from which a richer life and new freedoms can grow.

Chapter 15

Freedom and Destiny

I sat in my office with the sunlight outside fading into a thin dark evening. On my couch was the nervous young man with whom I had been working weekly for about seven months now. He had learned to get home on time by setting his watch and had fought other battles with himself. He is the type of discouraged child who gives up excuses only to substitute new ones. As soon as I had unhooked him from one, he had others to keep at bay the feeling of responsibility he so often avoided. His father sat quietly in a chair across from his son. This young man was in quite a bit of pain. He was trying to explain why it was no use studying for a biology test the next day. He seemed desperate to me.

"I can't explain it any better," he said. "Every time I try to read this book, something just takes my concentration away. I can't make myself learn this. Something just happens."

The father gave me a worried look. The boy glanced constantly at his father. "So, there is no use in studying further,

263

in trying a little more to learn biology, is that what you are saying?" I asked.

He shrugged his shoulders. "You are just going to have to get used to my bad grades. I can't help it. Something just grabs my mind, and I can't learn anything."

I thought to myself that after seven months of weaning him from his excuses, he offers this rather lame idea. How helpless this child must feel! I could sense a great deal of inner pressure on him. His father remained silent. The boy had his head bowed. I felt we were coming to the end, where he would either become very depressed or he would have a break-through.

I wondered what his father must be thinking right now. He was a very successful man. He had graduated from Rice University and his wife from the University of Texas. A younger sister was a straight A student. An older sister had graduated from high school in the top third of her class. This young man had better than average abilities to learn classroom material, yet he was a poor student and was about to do poorly on an exam once more. How discouraged this father must feel, I thought.

I turned my attention to the young man before me. "Read me a passage from your textbook so I can see what this problem is really all about."

The boy opened his text to the chapter he needed to study. He read a paragraph aloud. "Now," I said. "Close your book and tell me what you have just read."

He followed my instructions. He could not repeat any of the ideas in the paragraph. "I can't," he said. "Something prevents me from learning this stuff." He looked at his father when he said it.

"Read the paragraph once more," I instructed.

He did so.

"Now, close the book and summarize what you have just read."

Again, he tried but failed to remember anything he had just read.

"Read it again," I instructed patiently. "Only this time, when you close the book, use the words in the paragraph to summarize it."

This time when he closed his book, he was able to summarize the paragraph quite well. I had him read the next paragraph with the same instruction, to close the book afterward and use the science vocabulary of the paragraph he had just read to summarize the paragraph. He was able to summarize the second paragraph perfectly. I had him repeat the same thing for the next two paragraphs. Afterward, he was not only able to summarize the next two paragraphs, but upon my request, he summarized the paragraphs he had just read. I had him finish the entire section of nine paragraphs of text the same way. It was obvious he was learning the material. He paused at the end and looked at me.

"You were successful, weren't you?"

He agreed.

"So, what happened to that thing or whatever within you that took your concentration away when you tried to learn this stuff before? Did it bother you just now?"

"No," he said. He seemed to be even more upset than before.

I said, "Then what I suggest you do is go home and study for your biology test the same way you studied for it here, tonight. You have learned a whole section in just twenty minutes just now. And when you study this way, you can concentrate quite well."

The young man glared at his father, who had remained silent.

I continued, "And if you need him, I am sure your father would be glad to sit with you while you do this." I turned to the father, "You can even learn some biology in the deal, too." The father heartily consented to help his son.

But the son only glared harder at his father. Tears were forming in his eyes. In anger he practically yelled out, "You make me feel stupid. You don't understand. It won't matter how much I study. I'll still not do well on that test. I'll never be good enough, ever." He looked at his father, now, completely swept away by his emotion. "You just don't understand do you?" he cried. "I'll never be as good as you," he sobbed.

His father looked shocked. He did not know his son felt that way.

I said, "So, even if you study, you'll probably fail anyway, is that what you mean? You'll fail to be as good as your father wants you to be?"

He nodded.

I continued, "So, it is better to not even try, right? I mean, if you don't try and then fail, that's really a better thing, isn't it? The worst thing possible would be to try hard in school, and then if you fail, you'd only prove once and for all just how stupid you really are. Is that how you really feel?"

"Yes," he said through his tears. "I'll just never be good enough, so why try?"

I turned to the father. "So, the truth is known now. We know what's been behind all of his problems all this time. Your son needs you badly right now. We've finally hit pay dirt. We can start over from here."

Whenever you have been working with your underachieving child and you have established a positive parenting relationship with him and weaned him from enough excuses, you may eventually discover the inner heart of his troubles. He may reveal the core feelings, beliefs, motivations, values, and perceptions that lock him into the discouraging, self-defeating attitudes and behavior that cause him chronically to underachieve and artificially to close doors to his future. He may reveal his pain, his sense of helplessness, and his desperation behind his compulsively self-defeating behavior. There, at the core of your child's pain lie the tangled, gnarled roots of failure and a repetitively self-discouraging life. However, there lie also the seeds of a new hope. Those seeds lie dormant in a discouraged child until he gains insight into how he causes his pain and discovers within himself the capacity to choose differently in his life. To choose differently means he must develop a true freedom of choice from within himself to create a new destiny.

Freedom and destiny sound like such big ideas for the problems of underachievement. Yet, freedom and destiny are at the heart of the problem and the deep goals of real change. If done correctly, the steps in this book will hopefully lead a child to discover that he is inescapably responsible for making decisions that lead to success or to failure. In the Ten Step Program, he is being brought to the crossroads of decision over and over again so that he must confront the inescapable fact that he is choosing among different destinies when he stands at those crossroads. If he makes one choice, failure continues. If he makes another choice, success more likely will follow.

These decisions occur in small moments on a narrow stage. When the alarm goes off on his watch, the child in the previous chapters will either decide to be successful and go home on time, or he will decide to fail once more. The freedom is inescapable. His destiny is in his hands. His choices in that small moment of his life will alter his future or keep it the same. The same is true for all who are brought to such crossroads in life where freedom to choose can make for one destiny or another. Where choices are strung together over time, one's destiny unfolds as a result of those choices, and one either lives empowered by his freedom to choose or enslaved by choices made without awareness that choices were even being made. Big ideas, like freedom and destiny, live in the small moments that unravel over a lifetime.

If we are aware of our choices, then our destiny is of our own choosing. If we are unaware of our choices, then our destiny is still of our own choosing, we just do not have any knowledge in the matter. We are slaves to the unconscious motives and feelings that drive us. We are slaves to ourselves . . . perhaps one of the most devastating kinds of slavery.

Discouraged children live in a state of inner slavery. Their failures and underachievement are very consistent over time and circumstances. They defeat themselves at almost every turn, compulsively, almost as though they are addicted to the machinery of discouragement running uncontrolled within themselves. They do not know how it is that they fail; they do not know themselves. Therefore, it matters a great deal when we bring a discouraged child to the crossroads whether he is aware of his freedom to choose or not. Simply being brought over and over again to those crossroads of choice can make a huge difference in a discouraged child's life. Many discouraged children continue to choose underachievement and self-defeat even as the excuses and denial are slowly stripped away. If the parents remain steady, patient, and positive under these circumstances, the real troubles in their child's heart will be revealed both to them and their child. It is at this point that things can begin to change for the better.

The history of my work with discouraged underachievers is replete with adolescents and young adults who slowly begin to change by becoming aware of the emotional and motivational barricades to success, confronting choices, and increasing their inner freedom to choose different achievement destinies for themselves.

Early in my work with underachievers, I worked with a young man whom I shall call Steve. Steve was in the seventh grade at the time, and although he was very bright, he made poor grades in school. He never actually failed a class, he did make Fs some grading periods and his grades during a grading period fluctuated from As to Fs. He had all the other signs of a discouraged child, too. He was dependent in academic functioning, had low self-esteem, lacked follow-through, and had plenty of excuses to help him remain an underachiever.

Steve also had been diagnosed as having a learning disability. Although his ability with language was superior, his ability to handle visual designs and work with his hands were only average. When I saw him, he had spent a year in a special learning-disability clinic obtaining the skills to compensate for his weakness. The specialist at the learning clinic had told Steve's parents that he was ready to achieve in school: unfortunately, Steve's grades remained poor.

In our third session together, I asked Steve why he had failed almost every spelling test he had had in school up to that point. He calmly told me that he was learning disabled. The words would be in his head correctly, he explained, they just could not get to his hand when he needed them on a spelling test.

The only way I knew to unhook children from their excuses back then was to use what kids told me in an artistic and creative way. Although I believed Steve did have a learning disability, I suspected he was using it as an excuse. I asked him to write down all his classes on a piece of paper for me so that we could discuss his grades in those classes as well. He proceeded to write down, and spell correctly, all his other classes, including such hard words as "science" and "mathematics." When he handed me the paper with the words spelled correctly, I felt I had a way to wean him from his excuse. I feigned shock and wonderment. I asked him how in the world he was able to do this.

"What?" he asked me.

"This," I explained, and handed him back the sheet of paper with the words spelled correctly. "You spelled every one of these correctly. How did you do that? I thought you said you were learning disabled and the words in your head could not get down to your hand when you needed them!"

I had made such a big deal of this moment that Steve was actually astonished himself. I had ambushed him and he was emotionally unprepared for my reaction. He was startled and stuttered back an explanation.

"I guess I just write these down so much that they must have come down to my hand automatically."

"Ah!" I said. "So, you mean that if you write down your spelling words and practice them over and over again, you will be able to spell them correctly when you need to?"

My impression at the moment was that Steve was genuinely taken with this moment. He said, "I've never noticed that before. I think you're right. I guess I can do it."

Steve was my last appointment that night. I was told by his parents that he left my office, went home, and told his parents what he had discovered with me about his learning disability. He went to bed, got up the next day without studying anymore for a major spelling and vocabulary test in science the next morning in school. Previously, he had failed those tests because he could not spell technical words correctly. On this test, he made his first C.

This one moment taught me much about the nature of excuses in underachievers. The label of "learning disability" had affected Steve at the level of his self-concept. In my view, Steve had become emotionally blocked from even believing he could pass spelling tests and dreaded them. By unhooking him partially from the idea that his learning disability had prevented him from achieving, I had helped free him from a debilitating self-concept and expanded his freedom to respond to spelling tests more intelligently. His first C of the year was a result of being emotionally freer to respond, not because he had gone home and studied more for his exam. What this taught me was that a positive change in one's self-concept, one's ideas about oneself, could lead to better grades.

Unfortunately, there are few miracles in helping chronically discouraged kids change for the better. Dependency still was a problem for Steve. One six week's grading period, his grades in science and English soared, especially those grades having to do with spelling and vocabulary development. I asked him why he was doing so well, now. He replied, "Because my mother is helping me study." I decided to let his mother help him by leaving him alone to study more on his own. His grades in English and science took a nosedive from As to Cs and Ds. "What happened?" I asked him. "My mother's no longer helping me," he replied. Obviously, in Steve's mind, his mother bore more responsibility for his grades, both the good and the bad ones, than he bore.

Steve's dependency on his mother was not good, so I decided to involve his father in his study life and remove his mother completely. This was not easy for the mother, which taught me how parents become hooked emotionally into enabling their children to remain inappropriately dependent on them for both success and failure.

Steve was a Procrastinator type of underachiever, and his father and I met for several sessions and mapped out a strategy for handling his son emotionally. The father could not get mad at his son, but had to handle him with great care and patience, and with insistence that work be done. If she had to, Mom was to lock herself in her room during study time.

One fateful night, Steve had some history homework due the next day. He needed his father's help. Steve could not find the answers to any of the questions on a handout, even though he had read over the chapter several times looking for the answers. His father looked at the handout and the chapter his son was on. "The answers you need are in the book, son. You need to look at the chapter again."

At this point, Steve's emotions began to escalate. The teacher was obviously stupid for handing out the wrong questions. Why didn't his father want to help him anyway, when his son so desperately needed him? Steve called for his mother, but she would not come nor even acknowledge that he had called her. (Actually, she told me, she literally locked herself in her bathroom so she could prevent herself from going to her son.) Steve began to whine and complain that people expected the impossible out of him, that his father wanted him to fail and did not love him. When his father simply repeated that he should look once more at the assignment sheet, Steve flew into a rage. He fell to the floor kicking and screaming how he was going to fail and no one cared, no one loved him, and how he hated his father and mother. Tears rolled down his eyes and his breath came in short gasps.

The emotional storm passed in several minutes. As Steve calmed down, his father said, "You probably feel a lot better getting all that off your chest. What you need to do now is take this sheet and look at it closely once more."

Steve took the assignment sheet from his father's hand. "Read over it," his father instructed. Wiping tears from his eyes, Steve reread the top of the assignment sheet. "Oh!" he exclaimed sheepishly. "I'm on the wrong chapter in the book.

No wonder I couldn't find the answers." He confidently finished his history assignment in about thirty minutes.

Weaning underachievers from the inappropriate dependencies that discourage them from solving problems on their own often takes a great deal of patience and tolerance for suffering. The father, by holding firm but being kind, became aware of the emotional turmoil inside his son that dependency on his parents had hidden from him. When he had to act on his own, Steve's fears about himself and his need for dependency on his parents burst in an emotional display that could have brought forth punishment from his parents. The father wisely allowed his son to experience firsthand how all those painful emotions blocked him from solving easy problems on his own. If his parents would have said, "Look, silly, you're on the wrong page," Steve would not have discovered how desperate his emotions were and how they blocked him from independence. Steve learned a valuable lesson about himself that night, and so did his parents.

Steve finished the seventh grade with modest improvement in his grades, but much more aware of himself. He did have a setback toward the end of the year, when his grades precipitously fell once more. He finished with C averages in major subjects, whereas he had had a chance to finish with higher grades. At the time, I did not understand what had happened. If I had had the Ten Step Program developed fully, perhaps I would not have had to wait until the spring of his eighth grade year to discover what Steve's real problems with grades were.

As it was, Steve had an incredibly successful fall semester of his eighth grade year. He made the honor roll every six weeks independently of his parents' supervision. He also was showing and talking a great deal about how proud he was of himself. He even bragged about how he was no longer like those "dumb underachievers" in some of his classes. He even asked me several times, rhetorically, how he could have done so badly before. He was also beginning to share some of his thoughts and feelings more with his parents and me. He was doing so well, in fact, that I was only seeing him professionally about every two or three weeks. He finished the fall semester in January with all As and Bs. The spring semester began quite differently, however, with a major setback. We were not through yet.

The mid-grading period report came out in February, and Steve had progress reports in every academic class. He had homework he had failed to turn in and he had Fs in math and English and a low D in science. All other grades were low Cs. Clearly, something had gone wrong. Steve, his father, and I met late one evening to discuss his grades. This was to prove the final turning point in Steve's young life.

We first went over what had happened to produce the grades. It was clear to all of us that Steve had not been doing his work. I asked him, "Steve, what went through your mind, what thoughts did you have when you sat down to study at night, but then didn't do any of your work?" This is a pretty complex question that only kids who have been trained to introspect can answer. As he had been with me for a while, I felt he could answer this type of question. He did.

Steve replied, "I thought, 'I don't care about my grades.'"

The nice thing about working carefully with discouraged

children such as Steve is that one can build evidence from their own feelings that they do care about their achievement. All I had to do at that point to unhook him from that thought was state the obvious. "You know, Steve, that's simply not true," I said. "Why all last semester when you were making As and Bs in everything, you were very proud of yourself. You do care. You care very much."

"You're right," he said. "I do care. I don't like those grades."

I said, "I know you care. So there must have been something else, deeper, that you were thinking that led to your not doing your work." I noticed that Steve became very anxious suddenly.

"I don't want to get any older," he replied.

Now, theoretically, I had already come to believe that a fear of the future lay at the heart of chronic underachievement problems. I believed already that discouraged children underachieved partially because they were clinging to childhood patterns of emotion, dependency, and motivation. Yet, every child has a unique reason for being afraid of the future, and when I am dealing with the concrete individual before me, I am always looking for the unique content of that fear. I also believe in the use of humor to arrive at the basis for such irrational statements as Steve had uttered.

"You know, Steve," I said, "I know several people my age who are concerned about getting older, too. If they were convinced that failing in business would mean they could stay the same age forever, then some of them might really consider failing. Do you believe that failing will stop someone from getting older?"

I noticed that Steve became even more anxious, now. "No," he said. "It won't. I've got to get older."

"But if you continue to do what you are presently doing, you may fail the eighth grade," I said. Steve nodded in agreement. "Then what is so scary about going to the ninth grade that you would want to fail the eighth?"

What Steve said next came straight from his soul, and I knew we had hit pay dirt. He said, "I feel like a dandelion blown in the wind." He became very quiet.

Whenever a child uses metaphor to describe himself in answer to a question about his fears, we should pay the dearest attention to it. A dandelion is a fragile thing. When hit by the slightest puff of wind, the dandelion scatters about, blown wherever the wind happens to be going. Steve was telling us that he did not feel very strong as a person, that his identity was weak. I reflected back to him my understanding. "You mean that you feel very fragile, that you may not hold together under pressure." He nodded in agreement. "What is the pressure exactly that you fear?"

Steve's eyes were watering when he spoke next to his father. He had a confession to make. "Last year at the end of the seventh grade, I started running with some guys who were older. They smoked dope and I had some, too. I wanted to be popular. But I didn't really like them, and over the summer, I wasn't with them anymore. I haven't done anything like that since. But, I know them. They are failing the ninth grade, and I'm afraid that if I go to high school, I'll be with them again and they'll make me do things I don't want to do."

Steve did not feel strong enough to stand apart from peer pressures and say "no" to them. He needed approval too much. Failure was his way of avoiding the hard choices of the world of high school. As we continued to talk about his fears and standing up to capricious winds of peer pressures, I could sense Steve was already feeling stronger. Children many times find strength within themselves whenever they confess their hearts to a caring, sympathetic parent who can guide them. I told Steve that his father had become an expert in telling people "no" in his business, and I assigned Steve and his father to talk for the next two weeks about standing up to pressures.

Steve and his father left my office about nine-thirty that evening. At midnight, I got a call from my answering service that Steve's mother was worried as Steve and her husband had not yet come home. When I called her back, they had just walked in the door. They had been driving around talking all that time. When I next saw Steve at the end of the grading period, he had raised his Fs to a C and a B, and his Cs to Bs and As. "I'm back to normal," he told me. When I asked him about being a dandelion blown in the wind, he told me he was becoming more like an oak tree now.

Steve continued to do well in school, although I no longer felt it necessary to work professionally with him. Two years later, I did receive a phone call from his mother. She was upset and wanted my advice about Steve. She said he wanted to attend a military school. "Was this Steve's idea?" I asked her. "Oh, yes. He wants the challenge," she said. "I was just wondering if he was mature enough." I could not help but smile to myself. How many parents want to send their child to a military school because they are desperate to find an answer for the child's dependency and immaturity that they have failed to provide for him? Now this woman's child wants to leave home to test his mettle in military school.

I said to her, "Yes, I think he's mature enough. Let him go. I'm sure his wings will carry him." There was a heartbeat of silence on the other end of the line. "I guess so. That's what his father said," she replied.

As I developed and honed in the more systematic approach of the Ten Step Program, the issues of emotional impediments to freedom of choice and the development of individual responsibility came even more into focus. When I trained parents to use the approach, they became more knowledgeable and respectful of their children's difficulties. The true nature of their children's emotional impediments to developing motivation for achievement became clear to them, and many parents knew instinctively how to help their children.

One such case in which I involved the mother deeply in treatment was a sixteen-year-old sophomore in high school named Don. Don was a sensitive, rather passive young man with a good intellect and wit. His mother had divorced his father when Don was eight years old. Don's father moved to another city in Texas where he had remarried, had other children, and had become a successful attorney. Don's mother was a psychotherapist in town. Don was her only child.

Don had all the symptoms of a discouraged child. He was bright but made poor grades through a lack of effort and lack of motivation. He was not a bad kid nor a discipline problem, but he was very dependent in his work and needed individualized tutoring and attention to pass in school. In fact, his mother even hired college students she knew to help him study and get his work done. He still made poor grades.

Don, his mother, and I cycled through many potential solutions to his grade problems. None of these solutions worked very well because Don failed to follow through on them. Since Don wanted to do well and recognized his dependency, he and his mother decided to get rid of the tutor. To help him begin studying for algebra, his worst subject, Don agreed to call me when he started studying every evening. He was simply to leave a message with my answering service telling me the time he started studying and the time he finished. For a while, this scheme worked because he was embarrassed not to study. About a week later, Don quit calling. Procrastination became the major enemy of his life after that.

Don's mother worked in the evenings and often would not be able to get home to make him work until after eight o'clock. However something always seemed to come up to prevent him from getting started on time. Week after week, Don, his mother, and I continued going through the steps of the Ten Step Program over and over again, making concrete plans for one problem after another. In treatment sessions, Don would often become quite depressed and even cry over his procrastination. Sometimes he would become very shallow in session, baiting his mother with his remarks until she became so angry and discouraged she no longer wished to come to sessions with her son.

Don's dependency became painfully clear one rather eventful session, one which also revealed the true nature of his emotional blocks to independent achievement. His mother had returned to sessions again at my invitation, but during this one, she would only be an observer and not participate without my explicit direction. I was also concerned about Don's depression. Don had begun to talk to me more and more about his father, how he would rather be living with his father at this time in his life. Actually, his mother did not wish to block Don's desire to be with his father, but when Don was younger, he had moved to his father's house and then had to leave because of conflicts with the stepmother and his father and stepmother's children. Don's mother had taken him to psychotherapy after the divorce and believed the issues of the divorce were resolved. I suspected that Don's paralysis in school arose from inner turmoil centered upon the loss of his father, and if my suspicions proved correct, I wanted his mother there to explore these relationships more fully. I wanted her to understand things from her son's currently hidden perspectives. I did not know for sure if father loss was really his problem. I was confident that we all would soon find out.

Don had made another concrete plan to regulate his own behavior and take care of his schoolwork. He certainly was able to identify how painful not being in control of himself was and how discouraging he felt doing badly in school. Once again, his current plan was designed to help him overcome his procrastination. At six o'clock, after one of his favorite television shows had ended, he was to get up from his chair and turn off the television. Then he was to sit down and begin his homework before his mother got home at seven-thirty. This was especially important since he had an F in algebra and poor grades in other subjects, as well. We had actually cycled through this very moment for several weeks and I figured Don had no more excuses left. Usually, when a child has no more excuses left, the ghosts come out of the closet. I felt that whatever in Don was organizing his emotions and behavior would soon become clear to all of us.

With his mother sitting silently nearby, Don had to admit to me that he was unable to follow his plan. I performed a sequence analysis by asking for explicit details about what had happened. Don told me that he watched his favorite TV show, but when it ended, he just kept watching the TV. He did not even like the shows that were on. He did not get up to study until his mother got home. When I asked Don why he did not get up to turn off the television his mood immediately went down. His eyes watered. He said, "No one was there to turn off the television for me."

"You mean you could not get up on your own?" I asked.

"No," he replied.

I wanted to focus more on that moment of paralysis. He told me he wanted to get up, he just could not make himself move. "It was like something else made me stay there," he said. "I couldn't help myself. I need somebody to make me get up."

"Do you want your mother to make you?" I asked.

"No," he replied.

"Then who else is left in your life who could help you the most right now?" I asked him. "Who do you really want?"

Don became very quiet as tears began to roll down his cheeks. "If I mess up enough," he sobbed, "my father will come to help me."

Don's true suffering and blocks to independence emerged

even more clearly as the session continued. Don had been like a hurt child who hides in the closet crying, magically hoping his parents will realize he is missing and in trouble and hunt for him until they find him and soothe his pain. He was able to see the irrationality of his now exposed motivation for failure and paralysis in his life. Failure would not bring his father to him. He had to reach his father in other ways.

As future sessions unfolded, Don, his mother, and I discussed his feelings of loss concerning his father and realistic options concerning Don's having more access to his father. His grades began to improve as Don dealt more openly with his loss.

I was unable to finish this particular case because the mother and Don moved away to another city a few months after the school year ended. However, Don was able to come to realize that life with his father would not be a good alternative for him. He visited his father before our work together had to end, and he returned from that visit reassured that his father missed him and still loved him. He and his father made concrete plans to be together more often as time and circumstances permitted. Interestingly, the more Don discussed his feelings and desires for a closer relationship with his father and the more he moved realistically in his father's direction, the more motivated and independent he became in school and the easier his relationship became with his mother during the time I worked with them.

It is often surprising to parents and children alike (not to mention some psychotherapists) that what appears resolved in one stage of a child's life resurfaces in a later stage of development. My most common experience is the hunger adolescent males experience for an involved, caring father to guide them into manhood. Adolescent males, developing normally, will often reject female authority and make their mother's lives quite miserable in doing so. The problem we face as a civilization is that when the adolescent male begins to reject female authority, the father is most often absent as well. Absence can occur physically, of course, in single parent or mother-dominated families or in families where the father is gone on business much of the time. Absence may also occur, however, when the father is physically present but emotionally remote, either because his character contains a large amount of emotional stinginess, because he is too punitive and perfectionistic in demands, or because he is drunk on alcohol or drugs too much of the time. A stepfather, or in some cases, stepfathers, have not, in my experience, been able to fill the gaps left by the absent biological father because often the mother will not allow the stepfather to play the disciplinary role or the child himself will reject the stepfather as a father. Further, stepfathers themselves are busy and remote much of the time, too, and are ill-equipped to handle their chores as a substitute father figure.

I have no easy answers to the father hunger in adolescent males. When the father is present in the home, answers are easier to find because the father can work harder to reach his son and their relationship can be improved. In Don's case, I was able to help him understand what he was doing to retrieve his father and help him develop more realistic ideas. Fortunately, his father was able to respond, which did help Don.

In individual cases, answers may be found. Yet, I have also worked with the fathers of discouraged children and have learned that the fathers themselves had poor relationships with their fathers, who were ridiculed by their mothers, emotionally or physically remote, demanding and punitive, or addicted to alcohol. The fathers did not learn from their fathers how to be a father when their own children needed them. The "father" problems for discouraged children like Don need to be solved because the absent father forms a critical, negative emotional impact on the child's sense of reality and identity from which the motivation for success may develop.

Development of a child's sense of reality and identity lies at the heart of discouragement and chronic underachievement. In Steve's case, he had a great deal of doubts about himself and his ability to stand apart from peer pressures. His original conflicts involved dependency on his parents for normal functioning, specifically with his mother, and an erroneous belief that failure was an unalterable reality due to his learning disability. As treatment gradually weaned him from his erroneous belief about himself and from his dependency on his mother, Steve got closer to his father and became more aware of the true information about himself, his real abilities, fears, hopes, capacities, and how feeling states could disrupt achievement motivation in his life.

In Don's case, his need for his father lay hidden in his rejection of his mother's authority and in his passivity toward achievement. He had organized his behavior around the notion that if he failed enough, his father would come to help him. When he had to actually experience firsthand the real feelings he had previously kept at bay, he had enough information about himself to make real changes in his behavior and motivation in school.

Whenever children are able to experience their feelings, conflicts, and irrational motivations, they have a chance to grow more aware of themselves. Through this growth and self-awareness, they can connect with the sources within themselves of their failures, pain, successes, and joys. They have the ability to gain more control over themselves and their destiny. They are more likely to accept responsibility for themselves and become more realistic in their achievement drives.

Coming to the heart of a child's identity and sense of reality can provide a basis for a deeper change in the parents as well. Parents can gain a richer insight and deeper appreciation of their child's inner struggles. Through growth in awareness of their child, they can connect with the sources of failure and pain in their child and offer more effective help than when they are ignorant of the true sources of their child's troubles. Quite often, through understanding of their child's inner life, parents come to understand how they have inadvertently been aiding and abetting their child's failures and suffering instead of helping him find a way out.

I worked with one family who provide a good example of how coming to the heart sparks a profound change in the father, the mother, and the son. This particular young man was very bright, but only made good grades in nonacademic classes. In math, science, history, and English he had a consistent pattern of poor grades. He would do well for a while, but then he would fail to turn in work, make Fs on tests, and generally sabotage his grades until only a Herculean effort at the end of a grading period would give him the lowest possible C or D in the course. He never failed a class. Also, he managed to pull C averages in most of them. In fact, his father often remarked during the course of treatment whether we were making too big of a deal out of his son's grades. He would correctly point out that his son was a good kid and would probably do okay in the long run. What bothered him most was the self-sabotage; he wanted his son to really excel just once.

By unhooking his son from multiple excuses, I was able to get this young man to ask himself and me the same question over and over again, "Why am I doing this to myself? Why don't I just once really work and make As?" I always feel better when kids begin to ask themselves the right questions even though they cannot provide the answers right away.

When his son started asking himself these questions, I had the father join us in the treatment room. In this way, the father could hear his son's struggles and join in the effort to discover the answer. After ten sessions essentially repeating the same questions in different ways, this young man had a remarkable breakthrough and gained insight into the nature of his real problems.

I was exploring with him what it felt like to make As in school. As he talked about his feelings he became quiet and fell into a rather prolonged silence. Then he said he felt like he was "way out there by himself."

"Does it feel lonely out there?" I asked.

"Yes," he replied. "All by myself."

I asked him if being lonely was why he failed, and he surprised me with his answer.

He said, "No, I fail because I don't know who I am anymore." He went on to explain his feelings this way. "Do you know I have been told all my life that I am so smart that I can do anything I want to. I have felt that I have no limits. Do you know what it feels like to have no limits? It's frightening. So when I make As in my classes, I start feeling like I am way off in space by myself without any limits at all. That's when I start failing, and when I've failed enough, I now have limits. I know what to do. I work hard overcoming the failure until I pull it out and pass. I create my own limits."

His father and I spent the rest of the hour discussing how it feels to have limits. We all discussed the possibility of defining his limits by the demands of the achievement tasks at hand, by living only in the "here and now" until each task is completed. I knew this was an existential idea that was just a way of approaching the problem of limitations on oneself and life choices that could not provide an ultimate answer for this young man, but perhaps only a temporary one to get him through. In reality, I felt his problem was really learning to live beyond the confines of his family, of possibly surpassing his father's accomplishments in life, a possibility he was not yet ready for.

His father was very moved by his son's confessions during that session. He told me later that he felt a profound emotional connection with his son that he could not put into words. A few days after that session, I received a call from the boy's mother. It seems her husband tried to put into words his feelings, but could not do so. In fact, I tried, but I could not do so either. "I don't completely understand what happened," she said. "But it feels right whatever happened." A wise mother knows when to let go of trying to know everything that passes between her son and her husband.

I continued seeing this young man for several more months before ending treatment. However, he returned to see me for one session when he was a junior in high school. He told me that he was in an honors program. If he made As in honors classes, his grade point average for college would actually jump above the top A average due to the extra grade points added to an A made in advanced honors classes. He told me that the first grading period of his junior year, he made an 89 in every class, the highest B possible. He told me he felt strange about that, that the 89s were not just a coincidence. "Somehow, I created those grades just that way." The next grading period, he also made 89s in all of his subjects. This time, he told me, he knew that was no coincidence. He had created those grades just like he used to create the lowest Ds and Cs. "I am still struggling with artificial limits. I just wanted you to know I was still doing that. It's just that now I am at a higher level."

I received a graduation notice from him at the end of his senior year, and his mother told me he was attending the University of Texas in the fall. We discussed how college would be a challenge for him, and we both hoped he would do well.

I received another call from his mother when he finished his freshman year at the university. "I just wanted you to know about my son," she said. "Before he left for school he talked to me and my husband. He told us he was going to really go for it his freshman year. He wanted to see what he was made of. Well, he made all As. He has a 4.0 average, and he is very proud of himself."

It was nice to receive that phone call. He had reached down into the fullness of his courage to reach up to his potential. Only a lifetime of living can tell the full story of an individual's destiny. At least for now, perhaps this young man can begin to learn what the real limits of life are all about.

Chapter 16

Persistence and Faith

The parents in each of these cases discussed in this book, indeed, all of those discussed in this book and all those successful cases I and my colleagues have worked with over the years, were very pleased with the changes brought about in their children. Naturally, they would be. Yet, I must tell you that in many cases, including all those discussed in this book, the parents almost quit treatment before their child achieved the insight and changes I've discussed. Doubt was ever in the parent's mind because change in their children's behavior was not fast enough in coming. Each of these parents told me there was a period of time when they thought seriously about terminating treatment and giving up on this form of help. They made the decision to remain, and that commitment made all the difference in the world.

Faith sustained these doubtful parents. They could feel deep inside that the road they were on was the right one, but their commitment was tested by early lack of results in school. It is unfortunate that we have become such a bottom-line people.

We have become used to the idea of instant satisfaction of our desires and needs. We find it difficult, even as adults, to tolerate frustration and work for long-term solutions to long-term problems.

The parents discussed in this book and those over the years who have sustained their efforts in treatment almost always had a belief in the process they were engaged in. They knew they were dealing with fundamental feelings, values, perceptions, and motivations, and they had the faith that if such things were explored and developed long enough, then only good could come from that. In other words, they knew something was happening even if they were not entirely sure just what it was. Their commitment was enough to sustain them through the uncertain times, even if their faith in the process was very, very small.

When parents stand at the beginning of a journey of change, many have no idea what they are in for. They often ask questions and have thoughts that reflect their doubts. "Will change be permanent, or will we have to do this for years?" they ask. "Isn't this just normal for kids? Won't he just grow out of it?" Or, "What are we going to do next, he's still not turning in his homework."

Frankly, if parents cannot make a commitment based on their feelings of worth and value, no matter how much doubt exists, then why should they expect their children to make commitments to things they cannot yet see, but only feel as a potential within themselves? No discouraged child, no chronic underachiever can really understand the tremendous personal values of good grades and an education and how these things can change his life for the better in the future. Discouraged children have little faith and commitment to the future, which is partially why they avoid it in the present by avoiding achievement that would take them into the future with a greater number of choices. Underachievement limits their choices in the future just as it does in the present and, hence, limits their responsibility for themselves in that future. In a very real way, underachievers' doubts about themselves and a lack of commitment prevents them from accepting the guidance of their parents and other adults. They doubt so much that they are paralyzed in self-defeating behavior.

Doubt can be a teacher for us, but we should never allow doubt to be our leader. If faith is our leader, then shovel by shovel or even if we use spoons, we can move mountains or change a child.

Yet, I know that it seems like such a long way to travel from the moment a parent seeks help for their chronically discouraged and underachieving son or daughter, through the Ten Step Program, through unhooking all the excuses, through all the confrontations and the revelations and confessions of identity and change, through setbacks and disappointments, to the end where, formerly discouraged, helpless underachievers take responsibility and work to change their destiny. The journey of some children and their parents take longer than others. Some give up before they finish. There is doubt almost every step of the way. And there are no guarantees of success. But for those who persist, the payoff can be tremendously satisfying, and such payoffs make all the work and sacrifice worth it many times over. The payoff is priceless.

For you parents who have read this book and are just now reading these words, for you parents who are at the beginning of learning about your own child's inner soul wherein lies the sources of his pain and yours, for you parents who are often just as lost and discouraged as your child is, I leave you with this message of hope. If you but have the faith of a mustard seed in yours and your child's capacities to learn and change and in the processes I've explained in these pages, then you can move a mountain, too, or change your child. A mustard seed is only a small thing, after all.

Index

About the Author

Michael D. Whitley, Ph.D., is a clinical psychologist in Houston, Texas, specializing in motivational difficulties and behavioral problems of children, adolescents, and adults. Over twenty years in practice has provided Dr. Whitley with a unique understanding of this special area of human behavior and, as an author and lecturer, he has shared his insight with the public through books, personal seminars, PBS specials, and radio and television interviews.